Directing Single Camera Drama

Directing Single Camera Drama

Mike Crisp

ⓕ

K2 8DP
0801-2041
A division of Reed Educational and Professional Publishing Ltd

ℛ A member of the Reed Elsevier plc group

OXFORD BOSTON JOHANNESBURG
MELBOURNE NEW DELHI SINGAPORE

First published 1998

British Library Cataloguing in Publication Data
A catalogue record for this book is available from the British Library

Library of Congress Cataloguing in Publication Data
A catalogue record for this book is available from the Library of Congress

ISBN 0 240 51478 5

Typeset by Avocet Typeset, Brill, Aylesbury, Bucks
Printed and bound in Great Britain by MPG Books Ltd, Bodmin, Cornwall

Contents

Acknowledgements

I am grateful to Michael Norman and Jim Tysoe for kindly allowing the inclusion of their scripts. I would also like to thank the actors Warren Saire and Fiona Lawrence who posed for the specially shot stills which illustrate the text.

The learning process in film direction is a continuing one and after thirty years in the business I realize I have learnt many things from many people. It is, of course, impossible to name, or even remember, all of them but I would like to record my gratitude to at least some of them.

Film editors:	Adam Dawson
	Paddy Wilson
Film cameramen:	Laurie Rush
	Chris Seager
	John Howarth
Film recordist:	Bill Chesneau
Dubbing mixers:	Pat Whitacker
	Mike Nadazzo
Directors:	Ann Benson Eyles
	Paul Jordan
	John Thornicroft
	Ken Dodd
	Chuck Despins
Artists:	Ronnie Barker
	Christine Drummond
	Sara Coward
	Dick Emery
	Miles England
	Sheila Fay
	Peter Harding
	Desmond Eill
	Ken Jones
	Robert Lindsay
	Annie Tobin

Lynn Verral
Joan Walker
Stephen Dinsdale
Antony Johns

NOTE

Throughout this book the various persons involved are referred to as 'he'. This is simply for convenience and is intended to avoid continually reiterating the awkward phrase 'he or she'.

1 Introduction

When any event is recorded by a camera that image is stylized. The very act of photography reduces our three-dimensional world to a world of two dimensions. If the scene is captured by a motion picture camera then time, which is so inexorable in the three-dimensional world, becomes malleable – even cheatable. The loss of the third dimension endows the film maker with control over time. It may seem esoteric, even pretentious, but an appreciation of that basic truth is the foundation of all creative direction.

Stage and screen

The audience in the theatre can have its attention drawn to particular parts of the stage by all sorts of devices. The simplest would be to have parts of the stage in darkness and only those areas lit which the director wished his audience to notice. On a fully lit stage important action can be placed prominently down-stage centre, dominant characters can stand while the more submissive characters sit. Costume design, stage positions and the sheer charisma of leading players can, and will, work powerfully to draw the audience's attention. However, should an individual member of that audience be bored, or know someone in the cast, there is nothing to prevent him from casting his eyes over the background action – notice his friend is the second soldier on the left or notice that one of the chorus girls is fatter than the others. In short, whatever devices the theatre director may have employed, he has not got total control of what the audience sees.

Total control is only available to the screen director. In film and television the director can limit the audience's perception of a scene to precisely the desired framing, controlling not only the size of shot but also the angle of view and, most important of all, the exact point in time that the audience receives the information.

This control of time is the screen director's most powerful tool and an understanding of its use is essential if drama is to be satisfactorily filmed.

Essentials

We are now so familiar with the screen image that it seems ridiculous to read that, in 1897 when the Lumière Brothers opened the world's first commercial cinema, Parisians actually cowered in the seats and some ran for the door when they witnessed the shot of a train pulling into a station. In 1953, when Hollywood had a brief flirtation with 3D films, some moviegoers may have ducked when Vincent Price threw a knife straight at the camera but I doubt if any of them imagined that they were in the same danger that the Parisians of 1897 perceived themselves to be. All sorts of devices have been used to tickle the palates of jaded cinemagoers. ('Emmergo' even had plastic skeletons flying over the audience's head on wires.) The more sophisticated the audience becomes, the easier it is for new film makers to forget the most important truth of the cinema. The basic truth that a moving picture reduces our three-dimensional world to one of two dimensions, a world in which left is always left and right is always right. This is not true of the real world where left and right alter depending on the way you are looking. The human witness to a real incident sees that event in real time and from one point of view. If he wants to take a closer look or see the event from another angle then he moves to get a better look; but this takes time. It does not happen in a 25th of a second. In the two-dimensional world of the screen viewpoints and perspectives change, they are cut together – wide shot followed by a closer shot, then a close-up, then a close-up in the reverse direction. These would be images of hallucination in a real-time three-dimensional world but they are the standard fare of the most mundane TV programme! Early cinema contented itself with a single camera position to record events. It would be fascinating to know if an edited sequence would have been even more terrifying to the Lumière Brothers' first audience, or simply so confusing as to be dismissed. It may seem a peculiar form of pedantry to witter on about the two-dimensional screen image but over the years, as I have taught film direction to people with a wide range of backgrounds and talents, it has always amazed me how little this all-important truth has been considered. An acceptance of the limitations of the two-dimensional world brings with it an understanding of just how powerfully that screen world can be manipulated.

Preserving real time

Film makers are often so obsessed with the compression of time and with cinematic excitement that they fail to realize that one of the most important skills for the director of screen drama to acquire is the ability to shoot a simple dialogue scene. A five-minute scene played between two actors could take anything from two hours to two days to film – depending on the complexities of lighting, tracking and location difficulties. However, the audience must believe that the scene took place in the few minutes of real time that the scene takes to play on the screen. This is why continuity is so important. The continuity specialist on the set will be there to worry about whether the actor had his waistcoat buttoned up or not, or on which word he took off his glasses. This is one type of continuity – important, but only part of the many elements of continuity that must be correct if the real time taken to film to scene is to be credibly compressed into its 'playing time'. Continuity of lighting, sound and performance are equally as important, if more subtle, than the more jejeune consideration of whether the actor had his hat on or not.

Continuity and weather

Visitors to a drama shoot are often impressed or perplexed by the amount of lights, and therefore electricians, in use. It is particularly puzzling to the layman to see powerful lamps in use on an exterior shoot in bright sunlight. One of the reasons for this may well be to reduce the contrast levels of the scene (which we will talk about in a later chapter).

However, when lighting a single camera drama, the director of photography has continuity of light as one of the prime considerations. The point is that the sun moves and the weather changes. If the director hasn't the money to pay for a large lighting rig then he must be prepared to wait for matching conditions if the scene is ever going to edit together in a convincing fashion. In the feature film 'Becket' there is a scene which illustrates the point perfectly and acts as an awful warning to the impatient director.

About half-way through the film a key scene involves the meeting between Henry II and Becket on a French beach. The scene starts with a glorious wide shot of the sands as Becket (Richard Burton) and Henry II (Peter O'Toole) ride towards each other. The weather is perfect. There is not a cloud in the azure sky. Then the scene cuts to a close-up of O'Toole – the sun is still shining but the sky is full of a 'Constable' fluffy white clouds; worse is to come. The cut to Richard

Burton's close-up comes like a smack in the face as the sky behind him is grim with dark storm clouds. These three shots are edited together for the rest of the scene resulting in a completely unsatisfactory sequence. No way can an audience 'suspend disbelief' when confronted with such a blatant meteorological assertion of real time.

So what should the director have done? Well, either reshot Burton's close-ups later in the schedule against a clear sky or reshot the whole scene. Obviously both are costly options but the first one shouldn't have proved too difficult. The original shot was a slightly low angle, just a close-up of Becket on his horse, backed by the sky. It could have been reshot anywhere – you didn't really even need a horse – and O'Toole's lines could have been spoken off-camera by another actor.

Now any director who identifies with the difficult task that is screen acting might be appalled at the thought of resorting to such artificial devices to solve a continuity problem, but screen drama is all about creating a false reality and experienced screen actors appreciate the fact. Wherever possible the requirements of the actor should be given first consideration but there will be times when the actor has to do something unlikely and just put himself in the hands of the director and the technicians. What is, of course, most important is for the director to have built up a bond of trust with his cast so that the actor understands precisely why his close-up is being retaken in a totally different location (or any of the other circumstances that may arise).

Stanley Kubrick's 'Barry Lyndon' is a *tour de force* of lighting conditions. Some of the exteriors in the early part of the film are quite beautiful to behold. The patience required to wait for such perfect low sun with its resultant long shadows is all the more remarkable when you consider how short a time such conditions usually last. There are many magnificent skyscapes behind the Irish scenes in the film, but the novice film maker is well advised to analyse these shots carefully. Really dramatic skies change very fast and thus play havoc with continuity. In 'Barry Lyndon' the most dramatic skies are used only in simple sequences (one or two shots at the most). The director was then able to get the scene 'in the can' before the conditions changed.

Every new director wants their first single camera drama to be a world beater. They've seen dozens of great films from directors as diverse as Orson Welles and Quentin Tarantino and they want to be up there with the greats. And why not? It's a laudable ambition. As a young film maker the last thing you want is for some boring old sod like me to suck their teeth and drone out a whole lot of 'I wouldn't do that if I were you' advice. However, time and tide waiteth for no man and often 'screweth' the unwary film maker. A simple dialogue scene shot in the street can be ruined if suddenly the owner of one of the cars in the background drives it away – all of a sudden the backgrounds no longer match. The answer, of course, is to make sure that all the cars in the background belong to people on your unit. Then there's no problem. It's so obvious once you know, or more likely once you've made the mistake, for you'll never make it again. It is certainly worth shooting a few simple scenes before you try anything world beating because the restructuring of time is a complicated concept with which to come to terms, yet it is the essence of all screen directing. One BBC drama director was so determined to 'be real' that he insisted on a shot of the lead actor boarding the actual train from London to Rugby and seeing the train pull out of the station all in the same shot. Only as he said 'cut' did he realize he would not see his lead actor for at least another four hours – such is the vengeance of time (or in that case timetables)!

Screen essentials

There are several factors in the shooting of any scene of fiction that need to be respected if the scene is going to have a maximum impact on the audience. The scene:

- Must hold the audience's attention and impart all the necessary information for the audience to continue to understand the rest of the story.
- Must edit together in a believable way, be of sufficient duration and played/edited at a pace which enhances both it and the scenes which precede and succeed it.

These are very general points and may seem too obvious to bother with but, if we examine them, we can perhaps glean some important truths of technique.

The scene must hold the audience's attention

There can be no argument here – if the audience switches off, changes channel or leaves the cinema the director has failed. How do we hold the audience? Some old hands would say 'in three ways – close-ups, close-ups and close-ups'. There is a degree of truth in this. Close-ups are valuable currency in the cutting room but, like any currency, they are all too easily debased. More important than more close-ups is the dramatic placing of those close-ups within the scheme of the scene (or the whole film). However, the audience still needs a sense of involvement, especially if you have decided to be sparing with close-ups. In any case the position of the camera is a powerful catalyst to audience involvement. If two actors are talking to each other across a table and the camera is placed so that we see two profiles either side of the screen and a lot of table in the middle, the audience quickly feels disassociated from the action (see Figure 1.1). If the camera shoots the scene over each actor's shoulder (Figures 1.2 and 1.3) followed by the matching close-ups (Figures 1.4 and 1.5) then the audience immediately feels involved – the camera has placed them as part of the action. (Figure 1.1 has a very 'stage play' look about it.)

Figure 1.1 Two actors at a table with empty middle of screen.

You might argue that Figure 1.1 conveys a sense of confrontation and that if the scene is all about confrontation it is a more suitable image with which to represent the dramatic content of the scene. This is true but dangerous, as the audience-exclusion factor still applies. A sensible solution, should you wish to create that sense of distance between the two protagonists, would be to shoot the scene with the profile wide shot (Figure 1.1) and the two close-ups (Figures 1.4 and 1.5) using the wide shot at the start and end of the scene and maybe once or twice in the middle. This would convey the emotional distance between the characters but the inclusion of the close-ups would ensure the audience still felt involved in the situation.

Novice directors sometimes confuse the dramatic circumstance between the actors with what the audience needs to see. The thought is that because the characters are at odds with each other they will remain at a distance and that therefore the scene can only be played in long shot with a large amount of space visible between the two.

Figure 1.2 Over actor's shoulder shot   **Figure 1.3** Over actress's shoulder shot.

This is a mistake, as it confuses perspective of the character with that of the audience.

Again, like the table example, the audience may need to see that there is a distance between the two protagonists but once that distance is established the audience should become involved, and this means over-the-shoulder two-shots and close-ups. The convention is that each of these close-ups is the point of view of the other character. The camera should therefore be at the same height and on the same eyeline as each actor. One character may be dominant to the other in the scene and, as we know, a low camera angle will make that character seem dominant. However, if both characters are standing and one close-up is taken at eye level and the other one from a low angle the resulting intercut will look very ugly. If you require an actor to tower over the other then that is precisely what they should do. One should sit while the other stands or one should remain at ground level while the other ascends a few stairs, talks down from the balcony or from the church hall stage.

In any of those situations the low-angle close-up will have a justification and thus look entirely natural. It will accentuate the dominance of one character over another in a manner

Figure 1.4 Matching close-up of actor.

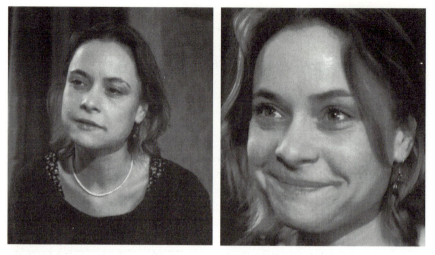

Figure 1.5 Matching close-up of actress.

Figure 1.6 Big close-up.

that develops unselfconsciously out of the way the scene is played. It should therefore be obvious that the direction of any screen play requires a synthesis of theatre and film technique. The low-angle close-up which would have screamed 'precocious technique' if both actors were standing at the same level passes almost unnoticed if the scene is staged in such a way that the dominant actor is playing on a higher level than the other.

Cutting to a close-up is most smoothly achieved if the close-up is the apparent point of view of one of the actors in the scene. The close-up of actor A is actor B's point of view of him and vice

Figure 1.7 Three-quarter establishing shot which 'involves' the viewer.

Figure 1.8 Flat-on shot which makes the viewer feel less involved.

versa. It therefore stands to reason that wide shots in the scene will be most easily accepted if they are three-quarters-on to the action and not flat-on to it. (Compare Figure 1.7 with Figure 1.8.) Generally it is unwise to place the camera 'flat-on' to a scene. The simple reason for this is that it emphasizes the screen's greatest weakness – the lack of three dimensions. Action towards and away from the lens causes the perspective of the shot to change – this is much more interesting to the eye and looks more three-dimensional.

If you need any further convincing just think of the difference between watching a classic Disney cartoon or a 1950s 'Tom and Jerry' and then viewing 'The Flintstones' or a 'Yogi Bear'. Hanna and Barbera, the animators of the original 'Tom and Jerry', realized that when television was introduced into the USA it would require a huge diet of cartoons. Now 'Tom and Jerry' cartoons have nothing like the complexity of moving background as a 'Snow White' or 'Pinocchio' but they do contain a lot of perspective animation – Tom chases Jerry 'away from or towards' the camera. This takes a long while to animate. The average 'Tom and Jerry' took 6 months to make. In creating 'Yogi Bear', 'The Flintstones' and the like, Hanna and Barbera simplified the animation process enormously using standardized leg, arm and head movements but the most cost-saving decision, and the one that makes the TV cartoons appear so poor by comparison with their big screen rivals, is that Yogi and Fred hardly ever walk towards the camera. The action is 99 per cent of the time across the lens. The animation therefore involves no changes of perspective and is thus about 70 per cent quicker to produce.

Of course, 'Yogi Bear', 'The Flintstones', 'Top Cat', etc. are enjoyable. They have a good deal of fun in them and memorable music and vocal characterizations. They are, however, undeniably, visually very poor relations indeed to 'Tom and Jerry'. The drama director should always have this comparison at the back of his mind. Live actors can move in any direction you like, in strong perspective at a diagonal to the lens or in dull perspective flat on to it. So you choose: do you want the visual strength of 'Pinocchio' or the pictorial impotence of those ghastly cartoons on children's TV on Saturday morning? They seem to have debased the art of pictorial story telling to such an extent as to make even 'Yogi Bear' seem akin to 'Alexander Nevsky'.

Close-ups – the basics

It seems I have strayed rather far from the theme of uses and abuses of the close-up but then in film-making the techniques interrelate so closely that digression is occasionally inevitable.

A basic truth is that you will never regret taking a close-up but will often kick yourself for not having taken one when you reach the editing stage of the production. You really do need to be aware of the danger of being talked out of taking a close-up by a reassuring cameraman. 'Honestly, Mike, we can see all that perfectly well in the two-shot.' When, in the cutting room, you can't see the vital detail at all you begin to wonder if the cameraman was deliberately trying to wreck the sequence.

The answer is, of course, that after seeing several rehearsals and shooting several takes he has had ample chance to see the close-up detail – hence his duff advice. The audience have only one chance – don't deny them that chance, take a close-up! Yes, that is very basic advice and seems redolent of those books on film technique that seem to wish to reduce film direction to a series of inflexible rules. Many great films have been made by iconoclasts who wanted to free themselves from convention but then many great films have also been made by traditional creators who rejoiced in their craft. As Lenin remarked, 'You can't make an omelette without breaking eggs but you can break eggs and not succeed in making an omelette.' Is the taking of our mandatory close-up so restricting to the film maker? Of course not! If we really feel that the scene works without it we simply don't use it. If, which I believe to be more likely, we do need it then it doesn't necessarily have to appear on-screen at the most obvious point in time.

Example

Our heroine visits the oppressive chief of police to ask for the where-abouts of her lover. The police chief denies all knowledge but says he will help her. She gives him a photo of the lover which the police chief puts in his desk drawer. In close-up we see that the papers refer-ring to the lover's arrest are also in the drawer so the audience needs to receive this information in close-up – but when? As soon as the lying police chief puts the photo in the drawer or later after the heroine has gone? The answer is that as long as the audience learns the truth then the best time for the close-up is at whichever point the director considers it to be most dramatically powerful. The cut to the close-up will need motivation, so perhaps after the heroine leaves our villain re-opens the drawer and only then do we see the arrest papers. He takes out the photo and throws it in the bin.

Lenses and angles for close-ups

Close-ups are generally best taken with a lens of reasonably long focal length. The portrait photographer knows this only too well when

Figure 1.9 Close-up with a long-focus lens.

Figure 1.10 Close-up with a wide-angle lens.

working on 35 mm where the standard lens has a focal length of 50 mm. The usual portrait lens to choose is between 75 mm and 135 mm. A long focal length softens the background and places the features of the face in their most flattering perspective. In cinematography the same holds true and close-ups taken with a wide-angle lens must be used with extreme caution as they distort the face in a very unkind fashion. OK for nightmares and horror sequences but not for romantic encounters. (Compare Figures 1.9 and 1.10.)

It is a general rule that the complementary close-ups in a sequence (actor A's view of actress B and her view of him) should be of a matching size and taken with a matching lens. Some of the real old die-hards in the industry would insist that the camera was exactly the same distance from each actor when their close-ups were filmed. Nowadays this is less strictly adhered to but there can be no doubt that 'matching singles', as these close-ups are often called, work best.

It is perhaps worth mentioning here one of the dangers that lurks for the novice film maker. As we know that the wide-angle lens renders a very ugly close-up of its subject we might think that a scene between two characters, one of whom fancies the other but whose feelings were, sadly, not reciprocated, might benefit by using non-matching close-ups. The close-ups of the adored young man could be idealized by using a long-focus lens. The close-ups of the young woman he finds so unattractive could be taken on a wide-angle lens to emphasize his distaste. This is technically true but proceed with caution because too wide a lens will cause such distortion as to confuse the audience and maybe provoke unwanted laughter. Most important of all is for the audience to realize that the close shots of the unfortunate characters are subjective, that they represent each character's view of the other. If this is quite clear from the plot and dialogue then such a device could well enhance the sequence, if not it will merely confuse. A most important discipline for any director to realize is that an idea does not communicate itself to the audience simply because it was in the director's head at the time of the shoot. Therefore in the example given above perhaps caution would be best observed – the romantic close-ups shot with a long-focus lens, but the unflattering close-ups shot with a standard lens, each close-up framed to be the same size. This would provide very 'plain' close-ups of the girl without shrieking 'technique' to the audience.

Figure 1.11 Two-shot using a wide-angle lens. Both actors are in focus. Notice the distortion which makes the actress seem bigger.

Figure 1.12 A longer focal length lens makes each artist seem of equal size but now the limited depth of field means that only one of them can be in focus.

Angles and close-ups

I have stated above that a low angle will always make the subject look more impressive and threatening. It will also make the subject appear less beautiful and this particularly applies to actors and actresses of middle age and above. A close-up from a slightly high angle can disguise the ravages of time around the neck and provide assistance to the ageing leading lady. Again these are purely pieces of information to bear in mind when planning your sequence. The overriding rule is that a close-up should match the eye line (height and direction) of the immediately preceding shot in the sequence.

Minimum cover

It is seldom that a director has more time than he needs to complete a sequence. In fact he is usually fighting the clock. A fallback position of basic minimum cover is a very useful technique to acquire. Any two-handed dialogue scene (two people sitting on a sofa, seated at a table, standing talking together) can be adequately covered in three shots; an over-the-shoulder two shot favouring the actor (Figure 1.13); a close-up of him (Figure 1.15) and a matching reverse close-up of the actress (Figure 1.14). These three shots provide ample cover for two to three pages of script typed dialogue. It is well to realize that when stuck for time you do *NOT* require the reverse two-shot (over the actor's shoulder). A close-up of the actress (Figure 1.14) is much more useful. The reason for this is that two-shot to two-shot is much more likely to fail because of bad continuity than close-up to close-up. You might be wondering which artist you should favour in the opening two-shot and the 'rule of thumb' is 'whichever one has the largest amount of dialogue'. That may sound terribly formula-ridden but it works and can provide a useful section of cover in a longer and more elaborate scene. Hero and heroine walk through the woods in a beautifully lit elaborate tracking shot, then sit on a log and converse. Once you've got them on the log the magic two-shot and two close-ups technique will work a treat. A word of warning! Those three shots are the *minimum* cover. A two-shot and a close-up of only one of the two actors looks very unbalanced when edited together and looks on-screen like the work of a very inexperienced director.

Close-ups are one of the most potent advantages that the cinema has over the theatre. Indeed many film historians will claim that 'The

Figure 1.13 Two-shot favouring actor.

Figure 1.14 Close-up of actress.

Figure 1.15 Matching close-up of actor.

Great Train Robbery' (*circa* 1905) is the first real dramatic story to be told in pictures as it was the first film to include close-ups. D. W. Griffith then went on to maximize the technique in the USA while directors like Abel Gance and Fritz Lang refined it in Europe. Close-ups are indeed powerful currency. Greta Garbo's first close-up in 'Anna Karenina' revealed, as the steam clears away on the railway station, a fine example of a star's entrance. Less self-conscious but equally effective is the tilt-up from the chess problem to reveal Humphrey Bogart as Rick in 'Casablanca'. The reason this looks much less self-conscious than Garbo's 'Karenina' entrance is simple. The camera for Bogart doesn't just tilt up to reveal him. It tilts up as his hand takes the cigarette from the ash try to his mouth. Motivated camera moves are always the least noticeable and usually the most effective. So close-ups capture and hold our attention. Some great films delay them as long as dramatically possible. This is a worthy cause but a dangerous one as nowadays so many films are made for television and its miserably small screen makes it the medium of the close-up. When directing for 'the telly' it is perhaps wiser to use close-ups in some profusion and hold some BCUs (big close-ups) in reserve for dramatic effect (Figure 1.6).

This section on holding the audience's attention has largely been about close-ups. There are, of course, other ways. An important one is to plan the shooting of a sequence so that as much of the movement as possible takes the action towards the camera. This technique overlaps into the next section so I will discuss it there.

The scene must edit together in a believable way

Whether we are shooting a sequence that vastly compresses real time (like a commercial), plays tricks with it (like a pop video) or purports to represent what is taking place on the screen as 'real time' (like a dialogue scene) the audience must always be satisfied with what they see. They must understand what they see and if they are puzzled then that puzzlement must eventually be resolved.

It is seldom sufficiently realized that one of the hardest skills for any screen director to attain is the ability to shoot a dialogue sequence quickly and efficiently. A shot containing two or more actors cutting to a similar size of shot which contains the same group will *hardly ever* cut together. The simplest example is two people on a sofa which, covered by two 'matching two-shot' camera positions, is perhaps the worst of all (Figure 16.1). The reason is that the continuity of the two actors seldom matches one with the other unless the scene is extremely tranquil and there is no shift of the actors' positions at all – no heads turning, no leaning forward and back, etc. Perhaps young directors are deceived by watching television situation comedies where matching two-shots are part of the regular, depressing, visual diet. The point is that sitcoms are recorded in a multi-camera studio and the cuts take place in real time as the vision mixer switches from camera 1 to camera 2. However, in a single camera operation several minutes or even hours may have elapsed between shot I and shot 2 and your edit hopes to reduce those minutes or hours to a 25th of a second. The solution to the problem is that of the minimum cover stated earlier, i.e. two-shot and two matching close-ups. It may seem as if I'm labouring the point but so many directors are talked into matching two-shots as sufficient cover by cameramen who should know better that I feel no shame in repeating *DON'T DO IT!*

If we accept that one two-shot cutting to another is a bad idea it is not difficult to visualize that if a two-shot develops into a single of one or other of the actors then the cut to the next shot will have a much greater chance of succeeding. If that cut is to a single of the other actor then we might be bold enough to suggest it cannot fail (unless the eye line is completely wrong or he's suddenly acquired a hat). Even if the cut is to another two-shot, remember that our first shot has developed from a two-shot to a single so the chances are that the cut will work. The change of image size often disguises any slight continuity errors that might appertain to the actor who is in

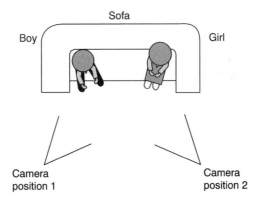

Figure 1.16 Two 'matching two-shot' camera positions.

both shots, i.e. the one who became the single when the first two-shot developed.

So, our two-shot has developed into a single but how? Well, the camera could track in or zoom into one actor and achieve a single. This is sometimes done but it can look very 'mannered'. It honestly only works in circumstances where the actor is saying something rather melodramatic – the sort of scene in which a ghost story is told or 'the curse of the Bunters' is revealed. In these quasi-comic situations the cut wide, which itself might look rather self-conscious, can often help the effect especially if the end of the yarn is mere bathos. However, 99 per cent of the time we want our development to the single to be achieved in a more subtle fashion. This is where the choreography of the scene (sometimes called 'blocking') is all-important. The technique, which once learnt is so useful to so many directors, is to choreograph a scene in such a way that the actors' movements around the set allow the shot to develop from a two-shot to a single.

Imagine that two actors are playing darts. As they throw they stand beside one another in an easily achievable two-shot. Then one of them goes to collect the darts from the dart board. This is the perfect opportunity for the two-shot to become a single. The camera either lets actor A leave frame as he crosses to collect his darts (thus leaving a single of actor B) or it pans with actor A and excludes actor B. I use the dartboard illustration simply because it is easy to visualize but the technique can be used in virtually any situation where one actor has a natural reason to leave the other one (crossing the room to the drinks cabinet, going to the cupboard – simply sitting down or getting up and moving to the door). Returning to our darts players we can quickly see how easily the sequence will edit if we see the two actors playing darts in a two-shot. The camera follows actor A as he collects the darts ending on a close-up of him by the board. He is talking back to his companion (so he can naturally throw lines over his shoulder towards camera). He collects his darts and walks out of frame back towards actor B. We now edit to a single of actor B and actor A enters this shot to reform the two-shot. Our original two-shot has thus developed into a single which has cut to a matching single which then becomes a two-shot again as actor B returns with his darts. This continuation allows enormous freedom at the editing stage and any dialogue sequence shot in such a fashion (two-shot develops to single then cuts to matching single which develops back to a two-shot) will simply fall together in the cutting room.

The question, of course, arises as to how we decided whether to follow actor A to the board or if it is better to let him go and leave actor B on-screen as our single. The answer must always be what is best for the story that is unfolding. If actor A is talking as he crosses then it is most likely that the camera should go with him. If actor B is talking and continues to talk as actor A crosses then the camera should usually stay on actor B. However, suppose actor B is talking but saying dialogue that is irritating or of particular interest to actor A. Then perhaps the camera should still follow actor A so that we can see his reaction to the dialogue. A film director has always to decide what the audience needs to see and then show them that clearly.

This is why directors who shoot their scenes from every conceivable angle and only decide how to put it all together in the cutting room are such wasteful charlatans. It would, of course, be possible to film our darts match using the device described over and over again to provide rushes of the scene which would easily cut; possible, but pretty dull. Here are two 'darts match' dialogue scenes and some suggestions as to how they might be directed.

TOM AND JACK ARE PLAYING DARTS IN A PUBLIC BAR. THEY STAND TOGETHER AS TOM PREPARES TO THROW. TOM IS SCREEN LEFT AND JACK SCREEN RIGHT.

TOM: Right this is it, suddenly I feel lucky. (HE THROWS)

JACK: One.

TOM: Shut up I can't concentrate. (HE THROWS AGAIN)

JACK: Three.

TOM: Blast!

JACK: Now suddenly I feel lucky.

TOM: Will you shut up! (HE GOES TO THROW AGAIN)

JACK: (AS TOM THROWS) Concentrate.

TIM: (AS HE THROWS) You did that on purpose –

JACK: Treble three!

TOM: I don't know why winning is so important to you. It's only a game after all.

JACK: Yes, it's just a game and I'm winning it!

Any screen director reading the script above will quickly note that Jack's last line is a strong remark which will benefit from being played in close-up. There are two ways of achieving this close-up.

Assuming that the majority of the scene is played in a two-shot of Tom and Jack then the last two lines of dialogue can be filmed in two ways:

1 Tom moves to collect his darts on his line 'I don't know why winning ... it's only a game' and as he moves the camera tracks with him to end in a single of him at the board. This will cut to a matching single of Jack for his punch line, 'Yes it's just a game and I'm winning it!'
2 The alternative method would be to direct Tom to leave the two-shot (towards the dart board) at the end of his line '... it's only a game after all.' The camera now remains with a single of Jack for the line, 'Yes it's just a game and I'm winning it.'

Is one version better than the other? With dialogue of such a basic nature it might seem precious to argue the point. However, I reckon that version 2 is slightly preferable. This is because it allows Tom to leave frame, which is an action more suited to losing character leaving the winner, Jack, triumphantly in shot. It also allows the next cut to be to Tom reacting to Jack's put-down and a reaction shot has more dramatic worth at this point in the scene.

Even a simple scene like this requires the director to have made up his mind how the shots will cut together before a frame is photographed. This becomes obvious when you consider the implications of Tom's move in the two different versions. In version 1 the camera will travel with Tom so he should start to move at the start of his line. *TOM: (MOVING TO COLLECT HIS DARTS) 'I don't know why winning is so important to you. It's only a game after all.'* In version 2 we need Tom in vision until the end of his line *'I don't know why winning is so important to you. It's only a game (HE MOVES OFF) after all' (THE CAMERA SETTLES ON JACK). JACK: 'Yes it's just a game and I'm winning it!'*

An important point to mention here is that if Tom and Jack are standing screen left and right respectively then Tom (standing screen left) should cross in front of Jack as he exits and thus exit screen right. This will look elegant as the camera reframes to form the single of Jack. Tom's move will take the viewer's eye in the same direction as the camera move. If Tom (standing screen left) exits screen left then the camera reframe on to Jack will appear ugly. The viewer's eye will be taken left by Tom's move but the camera will wrench attention to the right. Put in a nutshell, it is a 95 per cent rule that characters should not exit frame from the same side on which they are standing.

One final golden rule we can learn from our darts match example is that of changing actors' positions left and right on screen when-ever the opportunity arises. This is because in the two-dimensional screen world, characters' positions left and right of each other palls much more quickly than in the three-dimensional world of theatre. Therefore if Tom and Jack are standing screen left and right respectively at the start of the scene, if the scene continues when Tom returns with his darts he should stand to the left of Jack so as the scene continues Jack is screen left and Tom is screen right. A full description of the scene using our preferred version 2 would therefore play as follows:

TOM AND JACK ARE PLAYING DARTS IN A PUBLIC BAR. THEY STAND TOGETHER AS TOM PREPARES TO THROW. TOM IS SCREEN LEFT AND JACK SCREEN RIGHT.

TOM: Right this is it, suddenly I feel lucky. (HE THROWS)

JACK: One.

TOM: Shut up I can't concentrate. (HE THROWS AGAIN)

JACK: Three.

TOM: Blast!

*JACK: Now suddenly **I** feel luckily.*

TOM: Will you shut up! (HE GOES TO THROW AGAIN)

JACK: (AS TOM THROWS) Concentrate.

*TOM: You did that on **purpose**.*

JACK: Treble three.

*TOM: I don't know why **winning** is so important to you. It's only a... (HE MOVES OFF **TOWARDS** THE DARTS BOARD CROSSING IN FRONT OF JACK – THE CAMERA SETTLES ON A SINGLE OF JACK) ... game after all.*

JACK: Yes it's just a game and I'm winning it.

CUT TO REACTION SHOT SINGLE OF TOM AT THE BOARD. HE WALKS BACK TO JACK AND STANDS SCREEN RIGHT – JACK GOES TO THROW.

TOM: (AS HE THROWS) Oh look, there's Pete.

CHAPTER

2 Location filming

The chief difficulties with location filming are inevitably those of logistics – the parking of vehicles, the feeding and accommodation of the cast, the negotiation of facility fees for the use of each location, etc., etc. These are therefore the proper concerns of the producer and the production manager, and I deal with them in my book *The Practical Director*. However, while, budget permitting, the director can feel gloriously cocooned against the organizational nightmares that frequently beset location work, he will inevitably have his artistic concept adulterated if he decides on a completely impractical location. More artistic compromise will be forced on the director at a bad location than at a good one, so it is well to know what to look for as you search for yours.

Unwanted noise is the biggest waste of shooting time on any film for television so a location on an aircraft flight path is a very bad idea. Aircraft noise, of course, is completely unacceptable in a period drama and even if the piece is set in the present day, aircraft noise is still disastrous as any sound which vanishes on a picture cut is bound to be. A hero's close-up with the sound of an approaching jet which cuts to heroine's close-up with no jet on the track sounds ridiculous – and adding more aircraft noise to disguise the sound cut just makes the problem worse as achieving a match is impossible. It is worth bearing this point more generally in mind because one of the ways of disguising bad sound continuity in a much-edited sound track is to add more general background. The trouble is that if the dialogue is already recorded with a high level of background then adding even more is a pretty desperate ploy as it endangers the audibility of the dialogue. For the director to have maximum creative control over the final sound mix the dialogue tracks should ideally be as 'clean' (free from other sounds) as possible. Feature films get round the problem by simply rerecording all the dialogue after the shooting, but films for TV seldom have the budget to go to this very considerable expense of post-synchronization.

Thus a location like Syon Park on the western outskirts of London is hopeless as a drama location for a small-budget production because, beautiful though it is, it is flown over every 50 seconds by planes on the way into Heathrow. If you were prepared to post-synch then this would not matter, and indeed I have several times filmed dance sequences there, but these were all to playback sound, so we could ignore the planes.

Another important consideration for a location is size. Here theatre directors often make appalling mistakes. The scene is intimate, set in a small room – do we need to find a small room in which to film it? Logic would suggest this to be true but the two-dimensional world defies that logic. If a room is too small then the camera cannot get far enough from the subject to achieve even a simple two-shot unless it is fitted with a wide-angle lens, and what effect does a wide-angle lens have? It makes the room look bigger! The background is in sharp focus and there is no sense of intimacy. For this you require a long-focus lens but that only works at some considerable distance from the subject so you need quite a large room – and just shoot into one corner of it. Again as a rough guide you can always make a good-sized room look smaller than it is but you cannot make a small room seem as small as it actually is! To be honest if you were ever to film a piece set in the interior of a small terraced house the only way to get a real sense of claustrophobia would be to have the interiors built in a studio with the ability to lose the fourth wall as required. Only then will the cinematographer be able to select the best lens for each shot.

Let us assume that we are looking for a large country house for a period drama set in the mid-nineteenth century. What are the factors to consider?

First, of course, is the mood of piece. Is the house supposed to be welcoming ('Pride and Prejudice') or doomladen and sad ('Jane Eyre') or positively chilling ('Dracula', etc.)? Can we find one location that can provide two apparent locations in the script? Some country houses have a Gothic wing so Dracula's castle and Van Helsing's house might be different frontages of the same building. This might seem too much in the nature of a compromise for some directors yet I would argue that moving locations is a very time consuming and hence costly procedure. The advantage gained in extra shooting time from multiple-location use can really benefit a production. Extra time for rehearsal lighting and shooting are always beneficial. Unless he is lucky enough to be involved in the making of a 'budget no object' feature film, every director needs to have an inventive approach to location filming.

Let us suppose that the shooting schedule breaks down in such a way that on one day it would be convenient to film church exteriors in the morning and dialogue outside a novelty shop in the afternoon. We have found an ideal church but there is no novelty shop in the village. Perhaps the best solution is to 'dress' the most suitable shop window as a novelty shop rather than traipse miles to the nearest real location. In such a case part of the design team could work on the shop in the morning and have everything ready by the time the unit has finished shooting at the church.

The wonders of the computer 'paint box' are now available to supply parts of the scene that simply don't exist in reality. At one time the 'glass shot' would have been used to supply the castle on the hill, the simplest version of which was to have a skilled scenic artist paint an image on a large sheet of glass in front of the camera. The real landscape could be seen through the glass and a glass artist could cheat perspective and make it seem that the miniature painted on the glass was a distant castle on the hill (or whatever). Action such as cavalry galloping down the hill was perfectly possible as long as it did not cross behind the painted image. Nowadays, as I say, all this can be achieved in electronic post-production (even if you are working on film). It is costly but possible. Such processes really do allow one location to serve many purposes. An example of the old system being used in this fashion can be seen in the film 'The Dark Avenger', one of Errol Flynn's last swashbucklers. The film was made at Borehamwood where the MGM backlot still had the magnificent castle that had been built for 'Ivanhoe'. 'The Dark Avenger' script called for three separate castles and it was important for them to look distinctly different. The solution was the use of glass shots which added extra turrets or in one case much reduced the apparent size of the structure. Three castles for the price of two process shots!

The recce

Once the director has decided on a location the site must be visited by the principal technicians and production staff. At the very least there will be the director of photography, the sound recordist, the chief electrician (or gaffer), the designer, the production manager and often the grips (in charge of tracking devices and camera cranes). If there are stunts involved or special effects such as fire and explosions, these too will require a recce by the stunt co-ordinator and the effects designer.

Undoubtedly, however, it is the director of photography and the designer who are most in need of information at the recce. They need to know what exteriors you are planning to take and what interiors. If you are in the ballroom, do you plan to show all four walls? What is the widest angle you intend to take. Will there be a 'dead area' (i.e. a part of the room that the camera never sees) where equipment can be stored and lights can be set? Will there be night

exteriors? What is the mood of the various scenes – heavy with atmospheric shadows or light and cheerful? Should the ballroom appear to be lit by firelight, candlelight, gaslight, sunlight, moonlight, etc.? It may seem daunting but the more information you can accurately impart at this stage, the less things will cost. If the director of photography cannot be sure of what particular lighting effects you require he will over-order so as not to be caught out and the designer will order enough dressing props to furnish the whole room. If they can be certain that you will cover only a particular scene from three angles – as if it were a studio set with no fourth wall – then they will reduce their orders accordingly.

Showing the fourth wall

It is a useful discipline to think of your location interiors in the 'three-sided' fashion shown in Figure 2.1. If the action of a location interior encompasses all four walls of the room then the scene will take two or three times longer to shoot. If you set the action as if it was taking place on a stage it can be relatively quickly lit and shot. I hate the term 'master shot' (as mentioned later) but every scene should be set from a principal angle which contains most of the action.

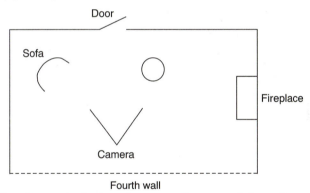

Figure 2.1 Shot from principal angle to contain most of the action.

Of course, that is not to say never show the fourth wall. The ability to do so is one of the most important advantages of single camera shooting over multi-camera work. However, if you minimize the number of fourth-wall reverse angles you will speed up your shooting rate no end.

Imagine a scene in which two characters enter a room and sit on the sofa and talk (Figure 2.2).

From camera position 1 we can easily take our actors (A and B) from the door to the sofa. From camera position 2 we can get an over-the-shoulder two-shot of actor A or a close-up of him. From

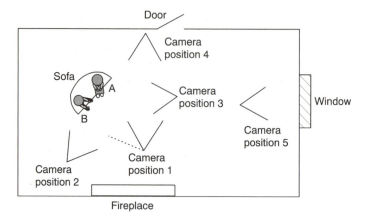

Figure 2.2 Minimizing the number of fourth-wall reverse angles.

camera position 3 we can get an over-the-shoulder two-shot favour-ing actress B or a close-up of her. At some point actress B might cross to the fireplace. If she does we will need to take the shots of her at the fireplace. From camera position 4 it will involve a total relight as we are now pointing the camera in exactly the opposite direction to camera position 1. If the action takes either or both our characters to the window then this will require camera position 5 and again need a relight. This is not a total reverse (as camera position 4) but it is likely to take time to light as if we can see daylight through the window and (if it is a sunny day) the contrast between the interior and exterior light levels will require to be balanced. This can be achieved either by fixing a filter material (scrim) to the outside of the windows (this is invisible to the camera) or by using additional light in the room or, most likely, a mixture of both.

This may all seem a bit daunting but it really is the sort of detail that the drama director needs to understand because if we are stuck for time then the scene can be most easily achieved if camera posi-tions 4 and 5 (the fireplace and the window) are only required to provide relatively tight shots, i.e. nothing wider than head to waist of the actor concerned. If this is the case then the relighting would not take much time and as far as the window is concerned not much will be seen through it, so it may not all have to be scrimmed.

It is also true that if the transition from camera position 1 to camera positions 4 or 5 takes place as an edit this greatly reduces the complexity of the lighting. If, however, you choose to direct the scene in such a way that the characters come in through the door and cross to look out of the window all in one shot the lighting would be much more difficult to achieve. If they then continue from the window to the fireplace (and you wanted to do this all in one shot) it would be very difficult indeed. Just ask yourself – where will the cameraman put the lights if the shot takes in all four walls?

One very useful time-saving technique on location (or in the studio for that matter) is to shoot all the fourth-wall reverses for any scenes that take place in the same set in one fell swoop. For example, imagine that two scenes (3 and 16) take place in the ballroom (Figure 2.3). Each of those scenes requires total reverse angles (cam positions A and B) and, of course, this means an extensive relight. Obviously it would be efficient to shoot all of the scene 3's 'cam pos A' lighting set-up and follow this with all the shots from scene 16 that require the same cam position and lighting – then relight the set and film scene 3's reverse angles (cam pos B) followed by those for scene 16. Working with his production manager a director might well 'fine tune' the scheme above. Maybe scene 16 is more complicated than scene 3, in which case it might be best to shoot scene 16's reverse angles immediately after the 'cam pos A' shots for scene 16 and leave scene 3's reverses to be last of all. Only a complete shooting script can provide the information on which such decisions can be made, which is why such scripts are so important.

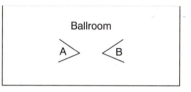

Figure 2.3 Shooting all the fourth-wall reverses for any scenes that take place in the same set.

Who decides what at the recce?

At the location recce the director's most important decision will be to agree that this is indeed artistically a suitable location. With luck, and experience, he will be able to state where and roughly how each of the scenes to be shot at this particular location will be directed for camera. He has to weigh up any sensible objections raised by the other people on the recce and decide if some small compromise on his part might not save vast quantities of time and money.

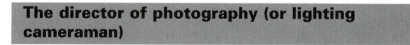

The director of photography (or lighting cameraman)

At the recce the director of photography (DP) discovers the director's intentions and then decides how much light and other special equipment will be required to achieve the desired effect. He decides if he can trust the director not to change his ideas between the recce and the shoot. If he gets a hunch that the director may well ask for many more complex shots at a later date, then the DP will 'over-order' to cover himself. Most particularly, he will want to know if there are any plans to do shots which start outside and track inside (or vice versa), as it is always difficult to balance exterior and interior exposures. If the director is planning shots for which it will be difficult to conceal the lights, the DP may well order up systems for suspending the lights rather than using floor-standing lamps. At the end of the recce the DP consults with the chief electrician (gaffer) about how many lights are required and what types they will be and this will determine the size of the generator(s).

The gaffer

At the recce the gaffer notes down all the various lights requested by the DP and often makes suggestions as to how one lamp may double for another (and thus save money). At the end he adds up the maximum amount of electricity (watts and amps) that may be required and orders an alternator or generator that is sufficiently powerful. He will also try to determine how many other lighting men (sparks) will be required. It is quite possible that more men will be required for the 'get in' and 'get out' than will be needed to run the location. However, too few men is not only a likely cause of injury but also might be a false economy. If by saving on one man (by having two sparks instead of three) everything takes twice as long to light then you are wasting money, not saving it. The gaffer will decide how he is going to get his cables from the generator into the building, so he needs to know what doorways and windows are likely to be in-shot. He can then find another one to use. The gaffer will also check out the local supply at smaller locations (or in small rooms at the large location) to see if it is possible to use this supply and save time on cabling from the generator.

A final point of discussion may be the desire to 'leapfrog' the lighting crew. It may well be useful to send some of the sparks off ahead to light a second location while the filming continues at the first. In such cases the lighting is rigged at the first location under the direction of the DP and the gaffer. The gaffer then leaves his assistant (or best boy) at the location with one or two sparks to work the set as he goes off with two others to rig lights at location B. He does this to a plan agreed by himself and the director of photography. This can be a very time-efficient method of work but it is labour-intensive. However, the film industry is much more flexible than it used to be. At one time if a film needed six sparks then it had them on the books throughout the shoot. Nowadays a core crew of three may be on the shoot every day with others coming in for a day (or a week) at a time.

The sound recordist

The recordist will usually have fewer immediate decisions to make at the recce but, even so, it is wise to have him along. Apart from anything else, the more key members of the crew who are familiar with the location, the better. The recordist will usually work with one assistant using a fish pole boom (see Glossary). However, certain scenes may require the use of radio mics or concealed microphones and, as these are an additional hire cost, the recordist will note what days these 'extras' are required. He will also advise on the use of playback facilities (for the ballroom scene) and these will often require an extra assistant. He will advise on the acoustic suitability of the location, though he will know from long-suffering experience that he will probably be ignored. However, if the plan is to use the corner of a large room and pass it off as a small one the recordist will check that the recorded sound will not give away the true size of the location. He will negotiate with the sparks to achieve a mutually satisfactory placing of the generator. The gaffer will want it as close to the set as possible to reduce cable runs while the recordist will want is as far away as possible to reduce 'rumble' on the sound track.

The recordist might also ask if the designer is planning to carpet the stairs/corridor/study, etc., as carpet will much reduce echoing footsteps and generally help in the recording of clean dialogue tracks.

Of course, if the recce is for the filming of a musical event (pop concert, symphony orchestra, the Three Tenors, etc.) then the recordist has as much, if not more, equipment to order and rig as the DP. This will consist of a mixing desk, foldback speakers and many and varied microphones and stands. The most crucial decision for the director of such musical extravaganzas will be whether or not the microphones can be in-shot. Frankly, if they cannot be, the overall music quality is likely to suffer.

The designer

The designer's (or art director's) job at the recce varies in complexity, depending on how much use is to be made of existing features and furniture at the location. It may well be that the staircase and hall furnishings of our location require very little alteration and all that is required is to add a few items of dressing and perhaps disguise a modern set of light switches with something more 'period'. It is also possible that only the structure of the interior is suitable and a massive amount of refurnishing, even repainting, is required. This has obvious consequences on the budget as the manpower and cost involved in safely removing and storing existing furniture and temporarily replacing it with quantities of hired items will be very high indeed. This is why it is so important for the director and the designer to be collaborative colleagues. If they agree on the feel of the film then the chances are that the director will select a location that is very nearly right and just needs some sensitive tweaking from the designer. However, it is possible that an empty neglected building can be hired at such a saving that the cost of furnishing it is economically viable.

The director and designer also need to agree between them exactly how far they are going to stick with period detail. For example, most parish church interiors have only looked the way they are now since about 1875. Before that they were either bare or more likely a clutter of seventeenth- and eighteenth-century private pews and galleries. Such original eighteenth-century interiors are now very hard to find. As few members of the audience know this the question arises – does it matter? As long as the church interior looks 'old' will anyone question it? There can be no right or wrong answer to such a question but I would suggest that if we were making a run-of-the-mill horror movie the 'olden days' philosophy might suffice; whereas if we were doing a piece like 'Tom Jones', which revolves around hierarchy, the visual statement of social division that squire pews powerfully represent should definitely be part of the scenic design. As an aside to such considerations I often wonder if the reason that 1930s films set in Victorian times always look more authentic to me is because there was more Victoriana left in the world then – or simply because in the 1930s there were still people around who remembered what it used to be like. It could, of course, be an impression of otherworldliness that comes from the age of the productions themselves.

The grips

The grips attends recces for major productions to advise on the possibilities of tracking shots and again to determine how many people his team will require. Most gripping can be done by one person working with occasional muscle power provided by the rest of the crew. Some large cranes require two or three grips and these will be booked by the day. Grips also advise on the safety considerations of

difficult tracking shots. On one BBC series about church architecture the grips at the recce saved a lot of grief by asking if there was a crypt under the floor of the nave. Had he not asked, the crane requested by the director would have crashed under its own sheer weight through the church floor!

The production manager

The person with the unenviable task of trying to extract as much information as possible from all the people on the recce is the production manager (or first assistant director). He will be noting all the various requirements, trying to contain these within the budget and, perhaps most important of all, trying to ensure that no-one is talking at cross-purposes. This often happens, especially if the director retreats into monosyllabic mumbles. Some directors do this in order to preserve an aura of creative mystery when the truth of the matter is that they are scared to death and unwilling to make decisions at this seemingly early stage. Two important points for the director to remember are that you have to make your mind up some time and that indecision fools no-one. It is for this reason that the production manager and director should visit the locations on a preliminary recce – without the rest of the team.

3 The director's role

Film making must be the most collaborative and co-operative of all the art forms, and I have always believed that the director should look on himself as a catalyst; the ingredient without which the actors in front of the camera and the crew behind it are unable to synthesize into a creative whole. So how does he achieve this? Well, every director has his own method. Some are egotistical monsters, some are quiet (yet hard as nails) control freaks. Some play dumb and get help from everybody, some are genuinely pleasant, creative people, some pride themselves on their efficiency but then are so committed to their visual scheme they leave no room for inspiration from actors or technicians. The list is endless, especially as many directors employ a complicated mixture of all the descriptions above in the course of their careers – sometimes even during the course of one film. It is probably therefore best to discuss what the various elements in the production require from a director and leave the individual reader to work out their own best method of approach.

The producer

The producer has overall financial control of the production. It is the producer who acquires the rights (if the film is based on a novel), commissions the script, persuades the star names to join the project and then hires the director. The director then takes over artistic control of the production but, though it is never mentioned, he is an employee of the producer just like the lowliest member of the cast or crew. I say it is never mentioned – that is the etiquette – of course, it is usually mentioned during the very first production row.

The director's first responsibility therefore is to the producer. The producer plans to bring a good piece of work to the screen and make a reasonable profit after paying all the bills. A conscientious producer will use some of that profit to finance another production. The director therefore is often honour-bound to bring the film in on budget. Every director wants to make his masterpiece but accepting a budget knowing that your visual scheme cannot possibly be realized on the money available is a pretty arrogant thing to do. However, as humility is seldom a director's strong suit, this happens all too often. When a director is well established he can often get his way even in the most dire circumstances of overspend, but it is not a wise plan for the first-time director to overspend. Indeed some financial, and indeed artistic, restraints often cajole the director to be at his most inventive and there are all too many sad instances of the producer, director and star being one and the same person. In these cases there are few restraints – and often few box-office returns either.

The star

It is unlikely, though not impossible, that an inexperienced director will work with a major international star. However, the director of modest fare for television will often encounter big names. The important thing is to strike the right balance between confidence and tact. All actors require a director so a show of undue subservience will cause more problems than it solves. On the other hand, most stars have very well-rehearsed routines to bring an over-assertive young director to heel (for example, Dame Edith Evans' 'If you're not careful young man I'll do precisely what you tell me'). It is important to remember that stars, like all actors, do not require to be told how to play the part. What they require is help in their search for characterization. If the actor and director agree on the elements that make the character 'tick' then there will be few disagreements on the set.

The actors

As stated above the director's proper function is to help the cast to find a creditable characterization of the part they have been cast to play. The most respected method is for actor and director to decide on the life story and experiences of the character prior to that part of his life that is dealt with in the script. Understanding the biography of the character is an enormous help to the actor's interpretation and of great help to the director in deciding on how the character will behave in any given situation. It is far more useful for actor and director to agree about why 'Billy Liar' tells lies rather than just try to get fun out of the fact that he *does* tell lies. If, for example, it is decided that Billy is a highly intelligent lad who desperately wants to change his lifestyle but hasn't got the courage to take action, his escape into lies and fantasy becomes easier to understand as well as giving a reason for the end of the play when he chickens out of his one real chance to break the mould. If a character is a drunk the director and the actor want to agree why he is a drunk. A good script will contain clues on which to work. The reason why Captain Mainwaring in 'Dad's Army' is a sympathetic character, despite the fact that he is often unsufferably pompous, is that over the many episodes we learn that he is an extremely hen-pecked husband.

'Dad's Army' is an extremely well-crafted piece of work in which all the characters are well rounded. The authors have provided cast and director with enough biography for each of them. You are not always so lucky and then the actor and director must come together to decide. Perhaps the character under discussion is similar to Captain Mannering – so perhaps it is helpful to decide that he too is hen-pecked at home.

It may seem to be rather slavishly following Stanislavsky to adopt the character technique when working on run-of-the-mill corporate video but I assure you it really can work wonders. I well remember working on a rather uninspiring training video for the Open University. The script made the teaching points clearly enough but there was not much character detail. The part of the company manager was particularly hard to bring to life as this rather vague figure drifted in and out with ever more contradictory information for his office team. Fortunately I had cast that consummate actor, Anthony Dawes, in the part and after half a day of rehearsal he said 'Trouble at home, I'd like to play it as if he has trouble at home.' 'Fine,' I said. 'Let's try it.' We did and it worked really well. If you consider such methods rather precious then do beware. They honestly do help actors in the creation of a role and it is the most barren scripts that require the most help.

Rehearsals

It is a sad truth that single camera drama is very seldom sufficiently rehearsed. Indeed some productions still call cast and crew to set on day one and start shooting with no rehearsal at all. I wonder if this tradition goes back to the days of the silent movie when the director could shout instructions at his cast while the camera was turning (a pastiche example of which can be seen in the film 'Singing in the Rain').

Some old-guard directors still choose to work without rehearsal. Maybe they feel that time for performances to develop will reduce their autonomy. Fortunately rehearsal time is increasingly being seen for the important value-for-money commodity that it is.

The director's approach to rehearsal is necessarily rather complex. He needs to have a very full knowledge of the script and understand the actions and motivations of the characters. He should have a strong overview of the atmosphere that is required on-screen for each scene, by that I mean the type of photography required, the look of the lighting, make-up, costume and, of course, the part that sound effects and music are going to play. However, he should not approach the actors like a puppeteer. For example if a scene starts with an actor and actress lying in bed in a dingy room, it won't matter to the artists who is on which side of the bed. If the actor has to get out of bed at some point (to get dressed and go to work?) the director should have a good idea at which point in the dialogue the move should occur. If the actor feels that the move to get dressed should be earlier or later, then the director should give such a suggestion serious consideration and, if it works with the timing of the rest of the scene, it would probably be best to go along with the actor's wishes.

It is well for a director to remember that he is not acting the scene – the actors are and if they are more comfortable with a move then the chances are it will look better on-screen simply because they will execute it with more confidence. If the director is really sure that *his* move is the best one then the job is to convince the actor that this is the case and do so by persuasive arguments. A director can only afford to be adamant if he knows the script inside out. Again it is worth repeating that rehearsals are not simply a process whereby the director drills his cast into ultimate submission but a period when cast and director are working to get the very best from the scene. The director provides the framework in which the actors explore possibilities under his guidance.

Reverting to the bedroom scene: the director has determined the lighting with the director of photography and the look of the room and the furnishings with the designer, he has decided which key lines will be played in close-up. Is it really worth a row about what line the actor uses to get out of bed?

But perhaps we are getting ahead of ourselves. The first thing that happens at any rehearsal is that the cast gather together for a read-through. This should be exactly that – an uninterrupted read, a chance for the actors to become familiar with the script and the other members of the cast with whom they will be working. The director should not interrupt the read-through – it should proceed from the start of the script to the end without a break. In fact it is best for the director to remain silent unless he chooses to read the stage directions that may be required for a full understanding of the scene. It is well to realize that a lot of actors hate read-throughs. They feel conscious that the director and other members of the cast may be judging them. For this reason a lot of actors give very little on the read-through and the inexperienced director may panic and wonder if the actors are going to be that 'flat' in actual performance. In fact, generally, the actors you need to worry about are those who tear into the read-through giving a bravura performance. They are likely to be the hardest to direct as they have already decided on their performance and will take a lot of persuading to change should the director not like it. Also they are in great danger of having peaked too early and it is therefore unlikely that they will have much to add to their on-screen performance.

It is quite possible that some film read-throughs will not have all the cast in attendance. Some smaller parts may well just be played by actors who arrive on set for one or two days. Even so, a read-through is still of enormous help as an icebreaker at rehearsals.

Blocking

Once the read-through is over then the blocking starts. This is the process whereby actors, script in hand, work with the director to find their positions on set and work out their movements and business in the scene. It is during the blocking that I believe that the wise director should be most flexible and tolerant. The actors are having a very difficult time; discovering truths about the characters they are playing, learning their moves and establishing a working relationship with other members of the cast. The director must be aware of this. It is well to have a good idea of the positions for the actors at the start of each scene. Joan is looking out of the window and Warren is working at his desk when Fiona enters from the hall. It is obviously sensible to have a plan in your mind (or on paper) as to how the scene will progress, but, as I have said earlier, an inflexible approach at this stage could well hinder the full potential of the scene. The actors may have some excellent ideas of their own. Of course, the director must have sufficient charisma to make it clear that his decision is final and you certainly do not want a situation to develop where one actor takes over or, worse still, where all the actors chip in with ever more contradictory opinions. Sometimes an actor will want to try some move or business that the director honestly believes to be quite wrong. Even so, let them try it! If you have an honest working relationship with that actor then one of two things will happen. After a few tries the actor will discover that he is wrong and should feel minimum embarrassment in admitting the fact. It is by no means inconceivable that after a few tries it becomes obvious that the actor is right and his idea is better than the director's. In this case the director should admit it. Too many directors feel threatened if their ideas are questioned. I think this is a bad mistake – as long as the director's overall concept is not under threat then any incidental idea should be welcomed as long as it is better than the one which it replaces.

Films are frequently rehearsed, if they are rehearsed at all, in rehearsal rooms away from the intended location. It is up to the director as to how detailed any of the rehearsal furniture needs to be.

A theatre play or play destined for the multi-camera TV studio needs to be rehearsed using furniture, as near as possible, the same size as that which will be used on the set. The shape of the set with windows and doors, etc. is marked on the floor with coloured marking tape. (The 'mark-up' is one of the television assistant floor manager's least glamorous jobs.) Frankly, a film can only be fully rehearsed on location or in the studio so I would question the need for a very full mark-up of the rehearsal room. What is important is for the actors and director to decide how they are going to tackle each scene when it is in front of the camera. If you are going to film a scene around the refectory table at Knebworth House, then in rehearsal you need a trestle table and some chairs and a knowledge of where the doors and windows are. A full-scale mark-up of the room would seem to me to be a waste of effort.

There is a huge difference between rehearsing for a play and rehearsing for a film. When the director finishes the rehearsals of a stage play, he and the cast must be confident that the performance can sustain night after night from curtain-up to the final scene reaching its internal climaxes of comedy, tragedy or whatever exactly as rehearsed. At the end of the rehearsals the piece should be polished and complete. I have never known this to be the case with a film, neither should it be. A film actor's performance should peak on the set (round about takes 2 or 3). The director is present to give final note before each shot and the actor knows that the speech will be filmed from a number of different angles. The whole mental attitude to the rehearsal process is, therefore, very different. For film it is more than sufficient at the end of rehearsals for the actors to be confident about their moves and motivation and reasonably secure with their lines. They should feel that there is plenty 'left to give' for the camera.

If a cast and director can work quickly to achieve good blocking for a scene this can pay dividends on location as the crew cannot set about lighting the set until they have an idea of what is going to happen. The ideal working method is therefore to aim to complete the filming of the scene at a reasonable hour (say 18.30 hours) then wrap the crew but work on with the actors for another hour to block the next day's scene. At 09.30 the next day you can call the actors out of make-up and costume to run the scene that you blocked the previous evening. Once the director of photography has seen the block he can start to light the set and the actors can return to complete their make-up. This is a very important point. Far too many directors wait until the actors are fully costumed and made up before bringing them to the set. If this is for a new scene it is an appalling waste of time as the director of photography can do nothing until he has looked at the scene. Then the actors can do nothing until he has lit it, so they just sit around getting hot and ruffled. By the time the scene is lit they will probably need to return to costume and make-up before they look fresh enough to start shooting. All this is avoided if you run the scene before the actors are fully made up and return them to costume and make-up to complete while the lighting takes place.

David Lean would often remind an actor that a camera can see what a performer is thinking, which was a tactful way of requesting a less expansive performance. It is certainly wise for the director new to single camera to think twice before asking an experienced screen actor to 'give a bit more'. I well remember directing a Gothic piece, all werewolves and bodies in the belfry, in which we were fortunate enough to have George Baker starring as the head of the doom-laden family. I left the set after day one convinced that I would have to ask George to bring his performance up a bit, but fortunately I had the sense not to say anything to him until I had seen the rushes. Next morning when I saw the performance on screen I realized that, of course, George had judged his performance level exactly right and if anything it would be best to ask the other members of the cast to bring their performances 'down'.

Rushes

Two lessons can be learned from this. The first is not to easily dismiss the experience of other colleagues on a film who have been working in the industry for much longer than you have yourself. The other is the importance of viewing the rushes every morning. This used to be standard practice in the heyday of the studios but often nowadays is let slip. Seeing the results of the previous day's work can save time and money as any shortcomings can be put right then and there. Film presents a problem with rushes on location and you may not get a daily service. Even so, it is a brave, some would say foolhardy, director who breaks location without having seen the material he has shot. Video has the advantage of being available for viewing immediately and film cameras with video assist also allow a tape replay. It is very important to realize that while you can judge performance and camera moves, boom shadows, etc. using 'video assist' recordings you *cannot* judge the visual impact that the images will have on the processed film. This is because video finders fitted to film cameras are 'add-on' units designed to steal a small amount of light from the camera viewfinder and send it to a video chip which records a useful picture but a picture that in *no way whatever* equals the colour and contrast capabilities of colour negative film stock.

Who should be at the rushes?

The question arises exactly who should view the rushes? My advice would be as few people as possible – certainly, the director of photography and the camera operator, the set designer, make-up designer and costume designer, the sound recordist and the editor. Obviously, you, the director, and the producer will have to be asked (if he is around). That really is the ideal limit. Rushes viewing is not a party. If the footage is to be properly evaluated it needs a degree of quiet concentration. It is hard for the operator to say 'God, I never noticed that shadow' or make-up to exclaim 'look at that wig lace!' if the whole unit, down to the last bit part player, is present. If the film is going terribly well and there is a family atmosphere then perhaps arrange a viewing of selected rushes at some point but don't confuse this with the proper procedure.

It is always unwise to show rushes to an inexperienced corporate video producer who, despite all expostulations to the contrary, will never be able to imagine how the footage will look when it is cut together. Put them off until you have at least a rough cut to view. You might even then consider using the old film editor's trick of including a couple of really awful cuts (which are in fact very easy to correct). The producer will then notice these, ask for them to be altered and leave the cutting room in a warm glow of creative achievement. If they *don't* notice the duff edits then you know you are working with a no-hoper!

One final thought regarding film rushes is always to remember that they are printed (or, nowadays, transferred to Beta) at one light. They are *not* graded. This means that occasionally there is a shot on the rushes that appears much too light or too dark. It is a sign of inexperience to panic at this point. The thing to do is to ask the film editor to check with the labs that the shot will print up (or down). Ninety-five per cent of the time the answer will be 'yes' so you won't need to reshoot.

4 Sound

Any director who doubts the creative potential of the sound track should always remember what the little girl said when asked if she preferred plays on children's television or children's radio: 'Oh, radio,' she replied 'because the scenery is so much better.' The trouble is that it is all too easy to belittle the recordist's role on location. The actors are rehearsed, make-up and costume are happy (at last!). The shot is lit, everything is perfect and then we can just hear a plane approaching, so what should we do? Well the only answer is to wait until the damn thing has gone. Most good recordists will be very honest with the director about what they can 'get away with', so when the recordist says 'honestly, we can't go with that' you must believe him.

Dialogue track recorded with the minimum of background distraction will allow the maximum use of creative sound effects in the final mix. This often perplexes directors from a theatre background. For example, a scene in a crowded pub is best directed so that the background artists are animate but in fact making very little noise at all. The background sound should be recorded as a wild track and then combined with the dialogue at the final mix. 'But this must look so false' you may be thinking. Well, no! Not if you work out how to direct the scene correctly. For example, a pub scene starts with a wide shot of the crowded bar full of activity. Then, as Fred enters from the back, the extras can be making as much noise as they like. Fred advances to camera and sees Bill in a far corner; we cut to Bill and Fred enters frame forming a tight two-shot. It is this two-shot in which the dialogue will be spoken and as it is quite close very little of the background of the two-shot will be visible and therefore can be played in near-silence. The crowd noise to match that of the wide shot can be added later. The canny director might also spot another potential advantage of such working practice. If we suppose that there are only three wide shots in the whole of the pub scene:

1 When Fred enters

2 When Fred and Bill notice Mavis leaving with her new boyfriend
3 When Fred and Bill leave together

then we only need a pub full of extras for those three shots. They can be filmed first and most of the extras can be released. Just ten or so remain to 'people' the background of the close shots. Thus both sound recording and production accounting are well served. The technique of 'noise reduction' when taking close-up dialogue applies to a host of situations from conversations on the factory floor (equipment running in the establishing shots but most, if not all, switched off for the close-up dialogue) to conversations around stationary vehicles whose engines are supposedly running. They are, in fact, switched off and the tick-over sound is recorded as a separate wild track.

In all these circumstances the director may well have to remind the actors to deliver the dialogue as if it was being spoken against a loud background noise otherwise the final effect would appear false. Filming sequences during which music should be played (i.e. the ballroom, the disco, the parade passes by, etc.) are particularly problematic because if any music is recorded with the dialogue then that dialogue becomes uneditable with every sound cut resulting in an obvious break in the music. Disco is maybe not too much of a problem as once the dancers get a feel of the music they can carry on bopping with playback turned off. Ballroom sequences are more difficult as there is a greater need to keep in time. In such circumstances it is again best to shoot wide shots with the music playing for the crowd to dance to and shoot the dialogue of our hero and heroine with a well-rehearsed camera tracking with them shooting sufficiently close to disguise the fact that the waltz, or whatever, is hardly being danced at all. Some Hollywood directors had the two leading artists swaying but in fact static on a dolly with the camera so that camera and actors could glide across the crowded ballroom in an apparently effortless fashion.

Microphones

The vast majority of microphones used in single camera production are highly directional. They are very sensitive to sounds immediately in front of them but are almost dead to sounds that are behind them. Therefore if you are having to film on a location with a heavy background sound you should at least stage the action so that the dead end of the mic is pointed towards the sound source. Scenes in a school playground, for example, will be best if the camera is looking into the playground facing away from the busy road rather than looking out of the playground towards the busy road. Generally speaking, the microphone will point the same way as the camera. If the road is an important element in the atmosphere of the film it should still be possible to film the dialogue looking away from the road (Figure 4.1). A simple procedure would be to have the actors walk towards the camera, towards the road and time the walk so that the dialogue ends as they pass the camera. The camera can now pan with them to reveal the road and the microphone swings with the camera towards the road. This is fine, because while the dialogue was being spoken the dead end of the mic faced the traffic noise.

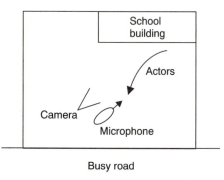

Figure 4.1 Microphone placement.

Directors sometimes mistakenly think that small personal micro-phones worn by the actors will solve background noise problems, the thought being that a microphone actually attached to the actor must be able to record good dialogue. There are three reasons why this is not true. First, small microphones can never be as good as their larger cousins; second, in a drama they have to be hidden under clothing so the sound is often muffled and prone to 'clothes rustle' and third, miniature microphones are omni-directional. They pick up sound from every direction so on a noisy location they are unlikely to record better than a highly directional 'gun mic'.

Personal mics are sometimes used to pick up sound from an actor who is deep in the back of a shot and out of the reach of the 'fish pole'. This can again cause problems because the sound perspective of the shot becomes inverted – in other words, the actor who is pic-torially the furthest away is aurally the nearest at hand.

A separate mic concealed on the set will usuallly provide a better aural match with the visual perspective in such cases. The recordist will sometimes ask a director if he intends to cover a particular speech in close-up. The reason for this is that the recordist knows that if that speech is a little 'off mic' in the wide shot it does not matter too much because the sound will be recorded again for the close-up take. If the close-up is not used for some reason that is no reason not to use the close-up sound – skilfully laid into the wide shot track it will replace the 'off mic' line easily enough. Just occasionally in a difficult location you will have a perfectly good take except that some distracting bang or crash occurred over a couple of lines. As long as the performances were otherwise satisfactory the situation may be possible to salvage by recording the lines which were spoiled immediately at the end of the take. The microphone will be in the same place so atmosphere and perspective will match. If you re-record the line as soon as possible after the take the actors' performances should also match and, again, the new line can be fitted to replace the one that was ruined by the off-stage noise.

Post-synchronization and history

When the directors of silent movies found themselves hamstrung by the introduction of talkies some just gave in to the new technology, others tried to find ways around the problem. When Warner Brothers filmed 'The Jazz Singer' in 1927 the noisy camera had to be imprisoned in a glass-fronted booth.

For several years this was the standard procedure – cameraman and camera shut in together in a cramped, soundproofed static box. The fact that it was static was the real problem. By the end of the silent era the camera had become a free-ranging spirit and feature film directors and cameramen then would vie with each other to achieve the most elaborate tracking shots. At first it seemed that sound had killed such visual adventures stone dead. Not only was the camera noise a problem. The Vitaphone recording system in use from 1927 to 1930 (approx.) recorded the sound on disc and this had devastating effects on the editing. Sound on disc locks the film into real time. Sure, you can cut away from your talking screen idol but only if the cutaway is exactly the same length as the footage it replaces. A frame more or less and the picture loses synchronization. For this reason 'The Jazz Singer' itself is an extraordinary film to see in its entirety. Al Jolson may have exclaimed 'you ain't heard nothing yet.' He might have added 'and you've never seen such a mishmash either.' To circumvent the impossible problem of combining sound tracks early Vitaphone films brazenly continued to use the dialogue screen titles of the silent cinema together with sound from the huge 78 rpm discs. So when our boy, Al, is singing on-stage and admiring Momma and Poppa in the audience turn to each other to say 'isn't he wonderful' they do so in subtitles. Meanwhile, Al sings on in glorious Vitaphone. Later Vitaphone films used two or three cameras – each in their separate booths placed around the set. They could film dialogue scenes from three angles at once, because they all ran synchronously with the one disc recorder. The output from the three cameras could then be edited together to make a complete scene but again it was stuck in real time.

The breakthrough that was needed was the ability to record the sound on something that could be edited with the same facility as the picture. By 1931 the Westrex recording system had fulfilled this need. By feeding the electrical output of the microphone to a glow lamp the Westrex recorder photographed the sound. Unexposed film passing in front of the glow lamp photographed its fluctuations so the microphone had turned variations in air pressure into variations of electric current and these variations had in turn been fed to the glow lamp. The variations in lamplight from the glow lamp were photographed by the optical sound recorder (or sound camera as it was properly called). The processed film was passed between a small lamp (called the exciter lamp) and a photo-electric cell. A photo-electric cell generates more or less current dependent on how much light hits it. These minute currents could then be amplified back into sound. The system became known as optical sound.

It seems extraordinary that it worked at all, but variations on this process provided the cinema with its voice for the next eighteen years. Indeed, even though now all film sound is recorded and mixed magnetically most cinema release prints have optical sound tracks.

At the same time as recording systems were being improved so were the cameras; or rather the camera cases. 'Blimps' were in general use by 1933. These were soundproof cases that fitted round the cameras releasing the camera and operator from the static box. So directors were getting close to the visual freedom they had enjoyed before the 'talkies'. Sound and picture could be edited and the camera was out of its ghastly booth. However, microphones were none too sensitive and the blimped camera was much more cumbersome that its noisy unblimped version. Recording sound synchronously with the picture was only really satisfactory if the film was made on one of the newly soundproofed studio sound stages. Directors like Fritz Lang and Reuben Mamoulion recaptured some of the freedom of their earlier silent films by shooting elaborate sequences in the old style and adding sound afterwards; post-synchronization as it came to be known. Indeed, Mamoulion was more innovative still. In his 1932 masterpiece 'Love Me Tonight' he recorded the sound of the complicated opening montage first and then shot and edited the picture to fit.

Even as late as 1935, MGM's 'A Tale of Two Cities' contained sequences that were in effect silent cinema with additional music and effects. These indeed are the most memorable scenes in the film and it comes as no surprise to learn that the film's director, Jack

Conway, had a long career in silent films behind him. He started out as an actor for D. W. Griffiths.

Technical knowledge

Does the modern director need to concern himself with such long-distant film history? Probably not, but the lessons that can be learned by observing how the most creative directors of the silent era adapted to the new era of the talkies are lessons that are timeless. In order to make the most of the new technology the directors of the 1930s had to at least understand the technical limitations of the processes they were directing. Then, like Mamoulion, they could devise ingenious methods of maximizing their creative potential. Nowadays each new development in sound and picture recording brings more freedom than restriction. Even so, it is wise for the director to keep abreast of developments and, where possible, use the technology in innovative ways.

A simple example in post-production sound would be the pitch-change device, or harmonizer. This was intended to enable the speed of a piece of music to be changed without affecting its pitch. Used discreetly, however, it can have a dramatic effect on the human voice, enabling, for example, a bit-part actor to sound much more resonant and 'Shakespearian' on film than he does in life.

Synch sound or post-synch?

It is obviously vital for the director to know at the outset of production whether or not the production is going to be post-synchronized or not. As a rule of thumb, most major international feature films are post-recorded. Most TV films and series are not. As a consequence, the boom-swinging and recording skills of the average 'made for TV' recordist are the highest in the industry. They have to be, because the sound recorded on location is going to be what the viewer will eventually hear.

If the production is going to be revoiced in post-production then the location recordist is in effect only supplying dialogue guide tracks. The boom is kept well out of frame so there is no danger of it coming into shot. It does not matter if the recorded voices are a little more distant or if there are occasional distracting noises which would usually render the take NG. All the actors are contracted for a considerable period after shooting to rerecord their dialogue. All this is extremely expensive so is the cost justified? The answer, of course, is yes, but the reason is not immediately obvious.

It is undoubtedly a huge benefit when shooting a film not to have to go again for sound. The joy of shooting a period drama and being able not to worry about a distant police siren or chainsaw is wonderful, but it is not that which has persuaded the major film maker to go down the 'post-synch' road. The fact is that 90 per cent of a feature film's audience will see the production in a language that is different from the one in which it was produced. Indeed the largest film audience in the world is in the Far East. To voice a film in another language it is first necessary to post-produce a sound track which contains all the sound effects and music required but with no dialogue (sometimes known as an M&E track). This is a long process, as every movement and noise must be recorded and matched to the picture, then combined with appropriate atmosphere tracks and music. The effect of seeing one of these sound creations being mixed with the picture is almost ghostly. Every sound you would expect to hear – door catches, passing cars, footsteps, dogs barking – is present but no human voice is heard. The point is that if you are going to go to all this trouble to facilitate revoicing the film in a variety of languages you may as well revoice it in the original language as well. Like every other sphere of production, the latest computer techniques have much simplified the once-tedious process of fitting the rerecorded voices to the picture.

Post-synch and the low-budget film

There may be some occasions when a production that was intended to use location synch sound throughout is forced to post-synch one or two scenes. Period scenes set in a London park will be impossible to record without anachronistic traffic noise, and this will also be the case at a number of stately homes. It is always best to decide to post-synch such sequences at the planning stages. Then budget can be set aside and the actors can be contracted for one or two days some three weeks after the end of shooting. If you leave it all to luck you will waste a lot of time on location waiting for sound and then when you are forced into a decision to revoice you may well find the actors are unavailable to rerecord their performances.

A number of other solutions may be possible. One is to very much limit the amount of dialogue that is spoken at the problem location. If that same dialogue is rerecorded at another, similar but quieter, location during the shooting period it should be perfectly possible for the editor to fit this dialogue to the picture. There is often a knee-jerk response to post-synchronization – that it must involve actors standing in front of a screen bravely trying to fit their words to the projected image. This is simply not true. The easiest way to record a few lines of post-synch is to have two recording machines. One plays back the actors original line and he listens to that line. Then immediately you record him repeating what he has just heard on the other recorder. Post-synch dialogue rerecorded like this will match the original in length, rhythm, inflection and intensity of performance. It should therefore be no problem to fit.

Interrupted dialogue

As long as the director has shown reasonable consideration to the recordist at the time of the shoot he really does not need to concern himself too much about the final sound track during the actual filming. As we have said, the quieter the location, the better; playback has its own special problems and any other difficulties will be advised to the director by the recordist as they occur.

One wrinkle that is worth knowing concerns rapid-fire dialogue. If two actors are talking over each other. As a required effect this is no problem in a two-shot – they can play it for real. However, if you cover the same section in close-up the actors *must not* talk over each other. That is not to say they won't appear to do so in the edited film. In fact, if you do let them talk over each other's close-up you won't be able to create the interruption. This seems perverse, but it is logical when you think about it. The *sound* that interrupts the close-up of actor A must come from the close-up shot of actor B. Otherwise when you cut to actor B the sound will not be in synchronization. In other words, the editor creates the interruption by laying actor B's close-up sound on another track before the end of actor A's speech. All that is necessary on location is for the actors to leave the briefest pause between their speeches and all can be edited easily. Sometimes you will hear a recordist say 'I think that line was a bit tight' – difficult to edit is what he means – but don't worry; experienced film actors will be used to being asked to ease off their delivery even if very few of them fully appreciate why.

Creative use of sound

If all the previous advice has been heeded then the director should be free to make maximum use of sound in the final production. Most directors nowadays are only too aware of the importance of sound, but if you have any doubts just try watching an action sequence or a Tom & Jerry cartoon with the sound turned down. It's not simply that the pictures are inadequate in themselves, it is because sound and picture together can deliver 110 per cent.

Atmosphere is as much conjured up by sound as by lighting and lenses. The door creak of the horror movie is nowadays almost too much of a cliché to consider but that is not to say that a door creak might not be a useful addition to a comedy – 'Monsieur Hulot's Holiday' contains a good example of that. The director needs to be imaginative in his use of additional sound effects. A passing distant steam train could be very effective in a domestic scene set in the 1940s or 1950s (even the early 1960s). In fact the nearer the piece is to the present day, the more useful sounds which draw attention to the period can be. Radio signature tunes ('Music While You Work', 'In Town Tonight', etc.) can be very effective albeit with a British audience old enough to remember the original programmes. The omission of such detail is all too easy for a director who has not experienced the era for himself. Office sounds, be they manual typewriter, electric typewriter or present-day word processor, are all key to a particular era so, even if the shot is merely of a character on the phone, the sounds from the unseen outer office can add period detail.

The list of possibilities of these general atmosphere tracks is virtually endless and I include these few samples simply to demonstrate that a scene usually benefits from additional sounds. All too often the only atmospheres that get added are the well-worn birdsong, thunder, crows, seagulls or sinister wind. All still very useful, but not the only tracks in existence! In any genre like horror, thriller or comedy, I would always be very cautious about using synch FX recorded with the picture. Gunshots are seldom sufficiently exciting and punches and slaps simply pathetic. They all need rerecording and refitting; broadswords are a prize example. Most prop swords sound about as dangerous as a couple of knitting needles. An FX recording session using two real swords that ring like a bell will add hugely to the feats of 'derring do'.

The 'Airplane' films provide excellent examples of upfront sound effects, again making the most of comedy. I will long remember the violent vomiting noises and the sound that accompanied the shot of the shit hitting the fan!

Reverberation (echo), often reduced to the slang term 'reverb', is an important weapon in the sound armoury. Footsteps which echo down the corridor seem of much more portent than those which don't. The door slam or banging the book down on the desk all gain with a touch of echo. The size of the interior, even what the walls are made of, can be suggested by adding echo at the mix. 'Adding at the mix' is the important point to note. Wherever possible, you should not record dialogue with echo already present as it can never be removed. In some locations (cathedrals, tombs, etc.) it is bound to be present but do not be surprised if the recordist tries to reduce echo on the original recordings as much as possible. It is then up to you to supply the discerned ideal amount at the final mix.

Sound, as a punctuation, is sometimes required by the writer but is another possibility for the director to consider. You know the sort of thing. The camera pans over idyllic countryside, we hear birdsong. At the end of the pan the camera settles on a corpse floating in a pond. There is a scream on the sound track which just precedes the picture cut to people screaming with pleasure on a fairground ride (or a steam train whistling as it comes out of a tunnel or an angry parrot in a cage). Yes, they are old tricks but they *do* still work.

One useful piece of self-discipline for the director to exercise is not to overload the sound track with too much detail. The analogy of a musical score is a good one. The most sparkling scores are those with a deal of separation between the various sections of the orchestra, the bass an octave removed from the middle and the treble well above that. The same is true of a final sound mix. We have mentioned the possibility of a passing steam train adding a period texture to a street scene. Well, if the date is 1900 so would the music from a barrel organ but to include both at the same time would be unwise. It is a good idea to think of the sound track as a sponge that can only absorb so much. Don't make the mistake of thinking that the wolf howling, a clap of thunder and an earsplitting crash from the music track will combine to give three times the effect. Sound recording does not work like that. Three loud effects at once can only be a third as loud as their maximum, otherwise the system overloads. Much more effective would be a clap of thunder followed by the wolf howl and then the orchestra crashes in. Used in this way each effect can be mixed in at maximum recording level and provide three dramatic effects instead of one disappointing noise.

It is often a good idea to start the music late in the sequence if that sequence has good loud sound effects to go with the picture. Battle scenes or fire scenes provide an obvious example. Let the gunfire establish itself and just before the effects track starts to pall bring the music in and you will achieve maximum effect. The battle scene in Orson Welles' memorable film 'The Chimes at Midnight' is well worth studying for all sorts of reasons but particularly its brilliant use of sound, and it very much adheres to the theory stated above. Much of the violence in 'The Chimes at Midnight' battle is in the sound and reinforces the point that sound focuses the attention of the audience. It can often provide the close-up you forgot to take!

Stereo

Feature films first started to experiment with stereo sound in the 1940s although the ever-innovative Abel Gance released his 1927 epic 'Napoleon' in 1935, this time with added stereophonic music and dialogue. The system used had been patented by André Debrie and Gance himself in 1932. Warner Brothers 'Santa Fe Trail' and 'Four Wives' (both 1940) were Hollywood's first stereophonic feature films, though most people mistakenly think of Walt Disney's 'Fantasia' (1941) as a stereophonic first.

'Fantasia', in its original form, is an interesting, if somewhat unsettling, experience for the modern student of film. This is because of Disney's delight in playing with his new audio toy. The orchestral sound image changes frequently during the film, sometimes within the same piece of music, so the audience gets a bit confused. 'Are the trumpets over there or over *there*?' When, in 1953, Twentieth Century Fox launched Cinemascope the original intention of studio boss, Spyros Skouros, was for every Cinemascope film to be released with stereophonic sound. It soon became evident that the cost of converting every cinema for wide-screen projection was expensive enough without the additional cost of installing a stereo sound system, so for a while stereo remained available only in the big-city picture palaces.

Television, in the UK, has gradually gone stereo but, as we know, many households still watch in glorious mono. This is a great pity from the drama director's point of view because stereo adds enormously to the production value and overall 'watchability' of a film. What impressed me when I first saw a demonstration was how much more the viewer's attention is held when sound is in stereo.

Stereo systems in use

There are two standard methods of recording stereo sound. One is called A/B and the other M&S. A/B stereo is a straightforward process which provides a faithful but fixed representation of the sound image that existed at the time of the recording. M&S is a much more flexible system which encodes sufficient information to allow a stereo mix at a later date but does not fix the positions of the various sounds. In other words, an orchestra recorded in A/B stereo will sound on playback just as it did in the concert hall – violins to the left, cellos to the right, violas and woodwind in the middle, etc. Should you want to alter the apparent 'sound stage' A/B won't let you. If you recorded the same orchestra M&S then you could virtually reposition the playback as you wished – cellos to the left, violins to the right. The system is not locked into the actual positions that existed at the time of the recording.

Fortunately, stereo sound for single camera television productions was being developed just before the brave new world of Birtism emasculated the BBC film department. There was at the time enough film recording experience left in the corporation to allow for the development of a very flexible and practical system. Recordists like Bill Chesneau (a leading light in the development of TV stereo) realized that stereo for a single camera production had to go down the M&S road. This is because it is not until the picture is fine cut that any decisions about stereo balance and perspective can be properly reached. Without wishing to get too academic about it, remember that often in a drama the picture will change to complete reverse cut but the sound will remain in its previous left/right split. If this seems confusing imagine our orchestra again. If we cut from a camera in the stalls to a camera at the back of the orchestra looking towards the conductor the picture has gone to a reverse angle. Instruments that were to the left of the first camera are to the right of the second, but only a fool would reverse the orchestral sound at the cut point.

Stereo sound is a great aset to a production. If it is properly mixed it lends not only a sense of left and right but also a feeling of depth (forward and back) to the picture. It doesn't require very much more time during the actual shoot, but a wise director will allow the recordist sufficient time to achieve really good atmosphere tracks. It does, however, require considerably more time to achieve the final sound mix. This is hardly surprising, as there are more decisions to be made than in the days of mono.

Stereo for feature films versus TV films

There is a difference to remember between mixing stereo for feature film cinema release and mixing it for television. The rule is that for television, if the object making the sound is in vision then it is placed in the centre of the sound image. This is the case for both close-ups or extreme wide shots. A wide shot of a train crossing a viaduct would place the sound centre-stage for as long as the locomotive was in vision. If the shot was of an empty viaduct onto which a train appeared screen-left and travelled across the frame until it disappeared screen-right then the mixer would allow us to hear the approach left and pan the sound to the centre as it appeared. He would mix it over to the right as the locomotive made its exit. This procedure would not have been adhered to in a feature film. The larger screen of the cinema allows for a left-to-right sound shift while the train is in vision.

5 Cinematography – what the director needs to know about it

When I was teaching film direction for BBC Television I was often amazed at how few of the student directors displayed any knowledge of, or interest in, photography. I was dismayed to learn that anyone should think themselves capable of being in creative control without any understanding of the basic process. It must be said that some of the worst offenders were theatre directors who were hoping to move over into the potentially more lucrative, but equally uncertain, world of films. If cinematography is a discipline that one has never investigated then I suppose it is all too easy to regard the process as nothing more complex than filming a play. Get a good script, a good cast, some interesting lighting and then point a camera at it. In all honesty, very few of the students had a concept as poor as that, but some did! The point is that even if you have an intelligent interest in the cinema and a strong visual imagination you are in danger of perpetual frustration until you get the basics under your belt.

A short list of hard truths for the director to understand is:

1 Any camera is much less efficient than the human eye, particularly when it comes to dealing with light and shade.
2 Unlike the human eye, the camera can be fitted with lenses of different focal length and these render a completely different mood to the shot.
3 You are reducing our three-dimensional world to one of two dimensions.
4 In losing the third dimension you gain control over time but only if continuity of performance, lighting and sound are sufficiently good to convince an increasingly critical audience.

Let us consider these points.

The eye is linked to the brain and, therefore, can interpret information. A movie camera cannot do this. It is dependent on either photochemistry (film) or electronics (video). Arguments about which type of image look the most real are therefore pointless as, in truth, neither of them do. It appears that most people find the image provided by film more pleasing than that recorded by video tape but the two rival systems are becoming ever closer in terms of aesthetics.

I mentioned earlier that both film and video are less capable of coping with contrast than the human eye and that what this means in practice is that, often, to create the effect that the eye would perceive, the director of photography has to light the scene in a fashion that appears wrong to the onlooker. The easiest way to get some comprehension of this is to take a few photographs indoors at home using not flashlight but lamps, if possible borrow a small set of film lights. If you light the subject from the side keeping as much spill as possible off the wall behind the model you will find that the developed photograph will have a well-exposed subject but the surroundings will go quickly off into darkness. The difference between the light levels of the lit and unlit areas which seemed slight to the eye at the time that the photos were taken will have been much exaggerated by the film process.

It is possible to buy a device called a pan glass which enables the user to look at a lit set and have some idea as to how the contrast of the scene will look on film. I would not recommend that a director flashes one too often on the set as such equipment is deemed the proper province of the cinematographer, but I would suggest you get hold of one and look at some everyday subjects through it. Once you get used to it you will soon see what the elements of film lighting are all about. Sometimes a director *will* say 'I want it to look real, I don't want to use lights at all.' Well, it is OK to shoot certain sequences without lights but I would question the use of the term 'real'. 'Grab it and run' news footage looks like it does because of a number of technical constraints. It is because we have come to associate those constraints with news footage that available-light shooting, often hand-held, has come to be regarded as spuriously truthful.

Let's consider why that style appears as it does. Whatever the lens, the depth of field gets less, the more you open up the aperture, so in dull conditions the depth of field for any lens is worse than in bright conditions. Depth of field is the term used to express how much of the picture in front and behind the subject will be in focus. Therefore if a cameraman is working quickly with little time to rehearse focus and he is using available light he will use a wide-angle lens, as a wide-angle lens will always have a greater depth of field than a long-focus lens *whatever* light is available. If he is working hand-held there is another very good reason for using a wide lens. The wide-angle lens decreases the effect of wobble and shake in hand-held operations (the corollary is that the long-focus lens exaggerates them).

This might all seem heavily academic stuff, but I stress the point because too few student directors realize when they make a pronouncement like 'Let's use available light and go hand-held' they are also dictating the type of lens that will be used. I don't wish to denegrate the use of wide-angle lenses. They are a vital part of any film maker's art but you need to understand that they have a powerful effect on the image. They exaggerate the size of the location. They throw objects near and far into sharp focus (which makes it impossible to isolate the subject) and they cause obvious distortion if used too close. So, if that is the look required, then working hand-held with available light will provide it. However, should you wish to create the mood of 'Amadeus', 'Emma' or 'Citizen Kane' then it definitely won't.

'Citizen Kane' is a much-written-about work and deservedly so. Its success must largely be due to the fact that Orson Welles spent three weeks with the great cameraman, Greg Toland, learning about film before they embarked on the project. Remember this was Welles' first film. This is the whole point. It is good, indeed vital, for a young film maker to have bold and original visual concepts but no use at all if they defy the laws of photography. In fact, 'Citizen Kane' does contain a number of deep-focus shots that seemed inexplicable. These are scenes in Xanadu and particularly in the opera house where, using a longish focus lens, Toland manages to keep foreground detail and background action in sharp focus. The most easily identifiable example is in the opera scene where the camera looks over the shoulder of Kane in his box down at the stage some considerable distance away. The depth of field of the lens in use makes it impossible for both Kane (foreground) and his wife on-stage (background) to be in focus, yet they are. So how was it done? The answer is by split screen. The shot was a combination of two exposures so the lens was able to focus on each half of the screen separately. It was very effective, seemed to defy possibility, and took time and thought to achieve. That is the essential point. If you are working 'low budget' and in a hurry, the effects available to you are those which obey the laws of physics, but that is not to say they should be used in a slavishly conventional way.

There are many books which will tell you the effects, pros and cons of using various lenses, lighting techniques, etc. My *The Practical Director*, also published by Focal Press, is one but the director of screen drama particularly is required to know the less obvious ramifications of deciding on a particular lens or effect. We have discussed how it is that using available light and going hand-held mandates the use of a wide-angle lens. The long-focus lens will, however, always require a steady camera mount, be that a tripod or a tracking dolly, and certainly the more light that is available, the fewer focus problems there are likely to be. A large amount of artificial light will be needed if you plan to track the camera from interior to exterior in one shot. Simply seeing out of the window to the scene beyond can be a problem on a bright day. Remember, the brighter it is outside, the more light is needed inside to balance the difference in contrast.

As the subject we are dealing with is photography it should come as no surprise that the amount and condition of light available can have an important effect on what is, or is not, possible to achieve. If directors don't understand the basics they often get confused (even ratty) when an effect that was easily achieved on one film proves difficult or impossible on another. It often is down to something as simple as whether the sun was shining or not. I think the reason that few cameramen ever really get to the bottom of the arguments that sometimes occur on the set is that such facts are second nature to them; so they don't ask sufficiently basic questions. 'Was the sun shining the last time you filmed here?' might well be the key to the misunderstanding. Here are some examples.

If you are filming in a large interior (a factory or a church) on a sunny day with a small lighting rig and the interior of the building is reasonably bright you may well be able to film someone coming in through the door and pan or track with them to see a large area inside (see Figure 5.1). The camera pans from position 1 to position 2 and enough light is coming through the windows for the cameraman to achieve a good exposure. He will use the few lamps he has available to brighten up any really dark areas of cam position 2.

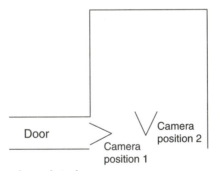

Figure 5.1 Filming in a large interior.

Should it be a dull day, however, the cameraman will need all the available light simply to achieve the entrance from camera position 1. He will not be able to pan to cam position 2 as it will simply be underexposed. The answer in this case would be to do the sequence in two shots. The actor exits cam pos 1 – there is a picture cut to cam pos 2 and he *enters* frame. In that way all the lights can be moved from pos 1 to pos 2 and sufficient exposure achieved. Of course, this might also have to happen on a bright day if the interior was a church with thick stained-glass windows and was dark inside despite the sunshine.

The shot described so far is quite simple. It only involves one actor – the focus is therefore no great problem as the focus can be pulled as he moves to keep him sharp. Suppose, however, there are two actors and as they enter one stays foreground and the other moves away from him and turns to talk back. Now we have a depth of field problem because even on a sunny day the cameraman using a basic lighting kit will be using a wide aperture. To achieve the depth of field required for the deep two-shot he needs a small aperture and this means he needs a lot of light. Continuing the example still further, suppose we are filming in the dark Gothic church with its wonderful stained glass. You, the director, require the effect of sepulchral gloom but you also require shots that need a great depth of field. The camera will therefore still need a lot of light, much more than the human eye requires. However, if the exposure is correct what will happen is that the interior of the church will still look dark and, importantly, the small aperture made possible by the considerable lighting resources will provide a great depth of field.

These are all further examples which show that the untutored eye can be no judge of what the effect on the screen will be. A complication that even some of the most experienced directors find perplexing is that the relationship between focal length and field of view varies depending on the size of the target area. In the case of film the 'target area' size can, as we know, be 8 mm, 16 mm, 35 mm or, in rare cases, 70 mm. What this means in practice is that a 28 mm lens gives a standard field of view if the negative size is 16 mm but is a wide-angle for 35 mm. Similarly 50 mm is a focal length which magnifies the image (i.e. is long focus) on 16 mm but is the standard lens for 35 mm. Expressed more simply, a 50 mm lens is standard for 35 mm, a 28 mm lens is standard for 16 mm and, remember, a standard lens is the one which as nearly as possible renders the scene as the human eye would perceive it.

Now we've already seen that the greater the focal length of the lens, the less the depth of field and this holds true whatever the gauge of film. So the standard lens on 35 mm has much less depth of field than the standard lens on 16 mm. If you are shooting in 35 mm you will encounter more depth of field considerations, the focus pulling is more demanding and generally you will need more light.

Steadicam

Hand-holding, though not impossible, is certainly more difficult on 35 mm than on 16 mm simply because of the additional size and weight of the camera. It was for this reason that the steadicam was devised. The steadicam is in effect a camera mount that is worn by the cameraman. The camera floats on a gyroscopically clamped head which the operator controls using hand-grip controls, like those on a motorcycle. Pan, tilt and focus are all achieved through these grips and the electronic viewfinder is used. The cameraman does not therefore need to put his eye to the viewfinder and the camera usually is positioned at about breast height approximately 2 feet in front of the user.

Steadicam operation is tiring and a specialist job. Most productions prefer to bring in an operator as and when they use the device. It can provide otherwise impossible camera moves but should never be regarded as a 'quick fix'. The device itself takes a while to set up and each shot requires a good deal of rehearsal. The steadicam is a prize example of a piece of equipment that may tempt a director to try shots with hidden difficulties. For example, a steadicam could be on the back of a troop lorry as it drives into the barracks. It could descend with the soldiers and run with them across the courtyard into the barracks, up the stairs and into the dormitory. The mechanics of such a shot are reasonably straightforward but what about lighting? On a sunny day the exposure differences between the cover of the lorry canopy, the open courtyard and the barrack interiors would be enormous. The interiors themselves would very likely have a range of exposures – staircases much darker than rooms with windows, etc. – so should we give up? Of course not; but we must realize that we have two choices. One is to use minimal lighting and alter the exposure as the conditions change. The other is to spend a lot of time and extra money using additional lamps to even out the exposure variations of the various lighting conditions within the shot.

The first option might seem the most attractive but remember that 'aperture pulls' (closing or opening the aperture to obtain the correct exposure) are always very noticeable and are particularly difficult on steadicam as the operator has enough to do without any additional problems. The second option is time consuming and probably made more difficult by the fact that the lights must not be seen by the camera. The longer the tracking shot, the more difficult this becomes. In fact I would dare to suggest that unless you are prepared to take time and trouble to light the shot properly it is hardly worth using the steadicam. If you are going for the 'aperture pull' method you might as well get a good hand-held cameraman, use a wide-angle lens and go for the earthy 'rough as an old boot' look. It could look really exciting. The steadicam is expensive to use and not to do it justice could spoil the ship for a ha'porth of tar. There is no right or wrong answer to the problem. What the director must appreciate is the complexity of the shot. Getting the camera from A to B is but a part of the overall technical obstacle to be overcome. You might be thinking that the shot in question might be more easily achieved on a cloudy day. My guess is you are right. The overall exposure variations on a dull day would certainly be less. The thing to remember is that in film making there is always more than one factor that determines how the actual cinematography is achieved and sometimes the hidden factors are the ones that prove to be the most time consuming.

Crossing the line

One of the most perplexing problems to confront a novice director is that of 'crossing the line'. The problem comes about because of the reduction of our three-dimensional world to one of only two. In a three-dimensional world left and right change depending on which way you are looking. The vicarage is to the left of the church if you are across the road looking at the church but to the vicar's right when he comes out of the church to walk home. In a two-dimensional world left is always left and right is always right. That is the problem. In an interview situation the line is between the two people's noses (see Figure 5.2). Shots from camera positions 1 and 2 do not cross the line, so the left-to-right relationship of the subjects remains the same. If the camera moves across the line to position 3, then subject B is no longer looking out of frame camera-left (as he is from camera positions 1 and 2) but is now looking out of frame camera-right. This geographical upset makes it unacceptable to edit shots taken from position 3 with shots taken from positions 1 and 2.

You *can* cross the line if the audience sees the camera travel from position 1 to position 3 because this reveals the change in screen left-

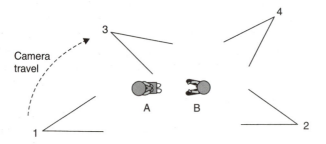

Figure 5.2 Crossing the line – an interview situation.

to-right geometry. However, after this change any subsequent shots of subject A will have to be taken from new camera position 4 in order to preserve the new screen geography.

The line may seem so obvious when dealing with an interview that you may wonder what all the fuss is about but beware! It is when actors start moving about the set that the problems occur (see Figure 5.3).

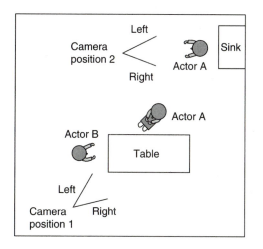

Figure 5.3 Crossing the line – when movement is required.

Actors A and B are chatting at the kitchen table. From camera position 1 the line is between their noses and actor A is looking out of frame camera-left. Actor A gets up and goes to the sink. You quite properly move the camera deep into the set to take his close-up (cam pos 2) as he leans against the sink talking back to actor B. But taking the camera deep into the set has *crossed* the line! If A was to take the true eye line to B he would now be looking out of frame camera-right which will not cut with shots taken from camera position 1. Though it seems strange, for the shots to cut, actor A still needs to look out of frame left when the camera is in position 2.

Dinner-table scenes are a nightmare for line crossing. Nearly every period drama of television has excruciating examples of line crossing if they contain a dinner-party scene. It really does matter because nothing is more disconcerting than watching shots of characters involved in an intimate conversation who apparently are not looking at each other. The important thing to remember is that if you seat the actors all round the dinner table then there is more than one 'line' waiting to ensnare you (see Figure 5.4).

There is a line between A and C and another between D and B. So shots of A, B and C from positions 1 and 2 will cut together because they don't cross the line between A and C but a close-up of C cannot

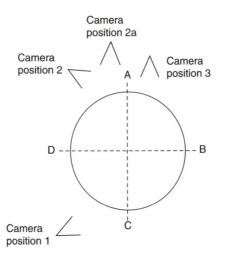

Figure 5.4 Shooting actors around a dinner table.

be taken from position 3 – it must be taken from position 2a. When planning such a scene it is best to draw a diagram such as Figure 5.4 and plan your shots so that no cut takes the camera across the line 'in play'. A simpler solution would be to reseat the actors as in Figure 5.5. Then there is only one line to worry about!

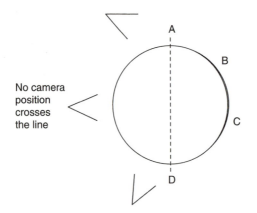

Figure 5.5 Reseating actors at table.

Summary

1 The focal length of the lens in use greatly alters the visual, and hence the emotional, effect of the shot.
2 Wide-angle lenses have a great depth of field. They exaggerate the distance between the subject and the lens, making distant objects seem further away than they are. The field of view is greater than

the human eye. Near objects appear distorted: with extreme wide-angle lenses they seem very distorted. Action towards a wide-angle lens seems faster than it actually is. Action across a wide-angle lens seems slower than it actually is. Wide-angle lenses are always used for hand-held shots.

3 Long-focus lenses have a limited depth of field. They magnify the image, so focus discrepancies and camera shake seem worse if you are using a long-focus lens. They provide a very attractive image with the subject in sharp focus against a more amorphous background. They are ideal for close-ups of hero and heroine. Long-focus lenses make distant objects seem nearer than they are and foreshorten the perspective, making objects close to camera, and those a distance from it, seem closer together. (Think of how short the pitch seems on televised cricket matches when a tele-photo lens is in use.) Action towards a long-focus lens seems slower than it actually is. Action across a long-focus lens seems faster than it is. Indeed to keep the subject in frame the camera will need to pan quite fast, blurring the background and adding to the sense of speed. A long-focus lens cannot be used for hand-held shots and requires a tripod or solid mobile mount for tracking, gibbing, etc.

4 The more light there is on the subject, the smaller the aperture that can be used. All lenses have a greater depth of field when 'stopped down' to a small aperture, but the wide-angle lens will still have a greater depth of field than a long-focus lens.

5 Contrast is a major concern to the cinematographer. A camera move from exterior to interior (or vice versa) will be difficult. An interior shot which starts looking into the room and then pans round to end up looking out of the window requires a lot of time to light and, on a sunny day, with a small lighting kit, may prove impossible.

6 Storyboards

Storyboarding is the process by which the director breaks down his sequence into the various shots which he draws on storyboard paper (see below). This is a really useful discipline as it helps to clear the mind when deciding exactly what it is the audience needs to see. It is also a very efficient way of communicating your ideas to the director of photography. If the shot is a track then the usual practice is to draw the first and last frames of the shot. The problem comes if you cannot draw – which indeed I can't! Then you have two options. One is to write a detailed shot list describing each shot as accurately as possible (the method I use) or on a grand production you can employ a storyboard artist who will provide a product that is often a work of art in itself. Using the specialist artist is standard procedure in the world of commercials where the client has to approve the concept and, as we all know, most such clients have the visual perception of a deaf bat.

Here is an incident and a suggested series of shots that will best convey the point of the scene:

'Kathy is walking across the courtyard between the two office blocks. A figure appears on the fire escape behind her. At first Kathy walks on then gradually she has a sense that she is being watched.'

That sort of screenplay 'stage direction' reads easily enough and is certainly possible to film. It may be interesting to consider various ways of filming the sequence and examine how one genre may differ from another. As it reads, the script extract could be describing an incident in a soap opera, a love story, a thriller or a comedy. The essence of the situation, 'Kathy walking across a courtyard becomes aware she is being watched', must come across whatever the style but the individual treatments will differ.

Version one

Shot number:

I Kathy walks across the courtyard towards the camera. In the background of the shot we can see the fire escape. As Kathy gets nearer a figure appears on the fire escape behind her. This shot requires a considerable depth of field and will have to be shot on a wide-angle lens.

II A close-up of the watching figure.

III Resume shot I – as Kathy gets ever closer we see in her eyes that she realizes she is being watched.

These three simple shots carry the message well enough but provide only a very bland sequence. There are no stylistic clues as to the relationship between the characters. At risk of causing great offence to some soap opera addicts I would suggest that it is a grudgingly adequate soap treatment.

Version two

Shot number:

I As per version one (Kathy to camera) but this time the camera is lower, lens about 3 ft 6 in. from the ground. The figure appears as per version one.

II The close-up of the watcher. The camera is slightly lower than his eyes to give a sense that he is looking down. It is *not* fitted with a wide lens.

III The watcher's point of view, i.e. a high angle of Kathy as she walks away from camera. The camera placed at the top of the fire escape. As this is a POV, it will require a moderately long-focus lens. Kathy would appear too small and insufficiently 'observed' if a wide-angle lens was used.

IV Kathy walks towards camera in medium close-up. The camera is at her eye level and tracks in front of her. It is fitted with the same long-focus lens as was used for shot III so the background around here is out of focus – we are very much in 'her world'. Kathy's expression changes as she senses she is being watched. The camera stops tracking, Kathy leaves frame and the camera pulls focus to 'the watcher'.

This version has elements of the thriller about it. Shot II (the watcher's POV of Kathy) certainly helps to make her seem vulnerable. However, the focus pull at the end of shot IV will not be visually as dramatic as it reads. Remember, Kathy is in medium close-up and the watcher is a distance away. As Kathy leaves frame the focus pull will reveal a small, unthreatening figure behind – visually more suited to a sad lovers' parting.

Version three

Shot number:

I As usual except that an even wider lens is used to lend an atmosphere of the surreal.
II The high shot looking down on Kathy, but this ends with a strong focus pull to reveal the watcher's hand foreground. Whether he is holding a weapon or not, the effect will be one of menace. To achieve maximum effect you will need minimum depth of field so that when Kathy is in focus at the start of the shot the hand foreground is an undecipherable blur, i.e. you'll be using a long-focus lens at a wide aperture.
III Tracking shot – Kathy towards camera in medium close-up.
IV Close-up – the watcher. A low angle and medium wide lens to add a sense of menace.

Version four

A comedy version of the sequence will contain the same types of shots as versions two and three. The differences will mainly be those of artist direction. For example, when the watcher appears in the back of shot I he will probably appear quickly, see Kathy and stop dead in his tracks in an ungainly fashion, rather than appear confidently. If we focus pull in the high shot it would be more effective to focus on the man's face looking really anxious in case he's spotted by Kathy. He would have to turn away from Kathy towards camera to achieve this. If we assume that in the comedy he was anxious to get away this would work. In version two 'the lover' and version 3 'the killer', the watcher would keep his eyes on Kathy and so to direct the actor to turn to camera simply to allow a focus pull to his face would look 'mannered'.

A final detail might be that in the comic version Kathy's attention could be attracted by the watcher accidentally knocking something noisily off the fire escape. A noise could attract her attention in the thriller version but the villain would not have much 'street cred' if he sent a milk bottle flying. A more sinister noise like the click of his flick knife or the creak of his leather jacket would be more suitable.

I have gone into reasonable detail with these various versions simply to illustrate that a simple four-shot sequence will benefit from storyboarding. The point is that you could 'knock off' the shots described on the day and you might cover the sequence completely differently, but if you storyboard you will know exactly the lens, angle and purpose required in each shot. So you won't waste time shooting too much cover and you will provide the editor with exactly the footage required to construct a telling sequence.

Getting the shot you want

Quite often you describe a shot to the cameraman and when you look through the finder (or at the monitor) the shot is what you described but it has not got the impact you had hoped for. This then is the time to consider if the right lens is in use. Would the shot be better if the camera was further away but zoomed in to contain the same framing, or is the shot improved by having the camera close to the subject but zoomed out? Either choice will alter the perspective of the shot and one of the two choices will be more like the image you conceived in your 'mind's eye'. Remember that for all that I have gone on about wide-angle and long-focus lenses, the zoom lens is a lens with a variable focal length. Zoomed fully out, it is a reasonable wide-angle, zoomed in, a considerable tele-photo. These provide the cameraman with a very flexible choice as he works. Should the shot require a lens that is outside the range of the zoom (i.e. wider than the zoom's widest or more magnification than its tightest) then the zoom lens can be replaced by other lenses. These will be prime lenses, that is, they cannot zoom but they offer a range of focal lengths outside the limits of the zoom lens. In practice you will find yourself replacing the zoom lens with lenses that are wider than its limit more often than fitting a lens that has a longer focal length than the zoom's longest. On 16 mm (nearly equivalent to Betacam) the standard zoom goes from a focal length of 10 mm (a reasonable wide-angle) to 100 mm (a good long-focus). It is therefore described as having a 10/1 'zoom ratio'. Quite frequently filming involves focal lengths of 9 mm or 5.9. These are outside the range and require the use of the 'prime lenses'.

The slap-happy shooting with no consideration as to the correct choice of 'focal length' can wreck an otherwise excellent work. All too often the reason why drama reconstruction on documentaries or schools programmes looks so poor is down to this. I recently saw a schools drama on the television about the Romans in Scotland. Quite a lot of money had been spent and the Roman Re-enactment Society had come along with about forty fully costumed soldiers. The director filmed all the shots of the army on the march using a wide-angle lens up close. This was a mistake as the depth of field clearly showed the empty background in nearly every shot. Had the 'army' been marching towards a long-focus lens with the camera about 50 yards away the effect would have been of a far greater number of troops. The reason why such productions nearly always look so cheap and false is 90 per cent of the time due to factors such as this.

7 Filming dance

Filming dance is rightly considered a specialist area yet it need hold no terrors as long as the director takes on board some basic techniques.

Filming dance with a single camera must be done to playback. Nowadays the supreme accuracy of the DAT audio players makes this much less complicated than of old. Even so, you need to have a playback master with time code prepared in advance of the shoot. If you are shooting 'beta' then this time code should be fed into the camera at the time of the shoot. The pictures will then automatically synch themselves up to the transferred master when you come to edit. If you are working on film you will need two DAT machines; one to record a guide track for each shot and the other to play back the sound. Again the playback master should be pre-time coded and the latest breed of film camera will record the synch information. The older cameras will still require you to use a clapper board at the front of each shot and, frankly, as the system is not yet foolproof it is wise to use a clapper board in any case. The point is that a DAT recorder will hold synchronization with the camera as both are so speed accurate nowadays. The time code link simply reduces the time it takes to match picture with playback sound. It is a huge time saver at the edit and should only be dispensed with in a real emergency.

If this all sounds a bit frighteningly technical, don't be too put off. The important thing for you as director is to let your cameraman and recordist know that you will be shooting to playback and make sure that the playback DAT master is time coded in advance. Leave the rest to them! The recordist may want to know how large the location is – simply so he can provide playback amplification that is of sufficient volume. Generally, dancers like it loud! One thing not to forget is the count in at the start of each number. This will enable the dancers to start their routine bang in synch with the start of the music. Sometimes the music mixer at the recording session has to be reminded of this as their usual procedure would be to edit out the count in when they record the master mix down.

It is often quite daunting when you first see a fast dance routine. It looks impossible to think of any way to cover it except in a wide master shot. I must admit that dance is the one area where shooting a master is valid. Don't be too tempted to go for a high angle. High angles are a safe way of containing the whole routine but they very much diminish the energy of the dance. A lowish camera with a wide angle usually provides better results. Unless the choreographer has had a lot of film experience you will find that the number has been staged to look good from the front. However, once you have seen it a couple of times look at it from the side and then see if any of the moves suggest a point at which you can cut to the side angle and then track the camera round to the front.

Ideally you should arrive at the shoot with a shooting plan that has broken the music down into various sections with the shot sizes and moves that are required for each section. As a very rough guide, a six-minute number will probably break down into four or five sections with maybe five or six details (tapping feet, hand movements, head turns) for close-up cover. You need to beware of close-ups when filming dance. As punctuation in a rhythmic number they can be both useful to the editor and artistically justifiable. However, dance is all about patterns and body lines. Nothing is more stupid than to film a ballerina on her points with her arms above her head as a mid-close-up of her face. To do so excludes both the vital elements of the dance (toes and hands). BBC 2 dance programmes of the early 1980s excelled in this crass type of direction. An arabesque shot from the wrong angle can look ugly, comic or both, and if you have any doubts be sensible and humble enough to ask the choreographer for advice. You cannot restage the whole dance but often dancing to a slightly different stage position or ending up at a better angle to the camera is much less of a problem for the dancers than you might think.

The best dance sequences are those in which the camera is choreographed in sympathy with the dance. Don't make the mistake of tracking in the same direction as the dance. This all too often kills any sense of movement within the dance itself. For example, if the dancers have a move in which they start in a group *upstage left* and then dance in a group to downstage right and then travel downstage left, the most likely camera direction would be to start with the camera *downstage right*. As the dancers cross to downstage right, the camera tracks towards the left, holding the group. When the dancers reach downstage right you can either hold the stage-left camera position, in which case the dancers will travel towards camera and you can isolate one of them into a close-up (which will allow for an easy edit to the next wide shot) or if the routine allows you can track the camera back to centre-stage and continue for a little longer. Whatever you decide, in most cases it is better for the dancers to 'chase the camera' rather than vice versa.

If the dance has sections during which it is static, tap dancing on the spot for example, it can look very exciting to track a low camera past the line of tapping feet and, if the camera move is timed to complete its track at the point where the dancers recommence their travels, the camera can widen to contain all this in an elegant shot.

Dances of all types often contain moments where one dancer after the other strikes an attitude on a rhythmic beat of the music. It is very effective if these attitudes are caught by the camera in a series of snappy pans or focus pulls or indeed a mixture of the two. Such moves will take some time to rehearse and if it is taking too much time, an easier approach would be to shoot these attitudes as separate close-ups. Whatever you do, don't fail to cover them all. It is always very unsatisfactory to watch a piece of dance where the music seems to be shouting out for a few close-up punctuations to the wide shots but they never appear.

The number of camera and rehearsal takes can be very tiring for the dancers. That is the reason for the sections. Make sure the recordist can find each section quickly and also make sure that the dancers know the musical points at which section starts and ends. If you are merely rehearsing for positions and camera moves the dancers should be told they can 'mark it', in other words go through the movements but cutting out exhausting kicks, splits, lifts, etc. A good director will let costume and make-up go in to make sure every dancer is looking fresh and beautiful before the take (they will in fact be tired and sweaty). Then remind artists and crew that this is a take. The sensible command for dance is 'Turn over and playback in 5-4-3-2-1 MUSIC!' A sense of melodrama is no bad thing if a group of dancers are about to give you three minutes of sheer energy (more so if it's to take four or five).

When editing dance it is vital that the synchronization between the music and the dancers is maintained. This seems so obvious that you might wonder why I mention it. However, editors are sometimes tempted to cut at some place other than the correct synch point (sometimes to rescue unsteady camera work or to avoid 'clipping' a focus pull or a zoom). The dance may still look OK to the untutored eye but the choreographer will go berserk! In such cases it is best to assemble the edit of the dance in synch complete with the dodgy camera moves and then find shots to cover over the offending footage.

Dance, like everything else, benefits from taking a few general cutaways; flashing lights if it's a disco sequence, mirror ball if a ballroom, etc. Classical ballet is more difficult as cutaways will appear to be just what they are. To avoid editing problems make sure that there is a reasonable overlap of the various sections and particularly ensure that the camera is steady at the point in each section where you intend to cut from one shot to the next. In really energetic numbers it is possible to create a very powerful effect by intercutting difficult sections (spins, Cossack steps, high kicks, etc.) with other sections of the dance from the other dancers. The effect created is that many more of the spins, etc. occurred than was actually the case. There is no doubt that the great advantage of single camera technique deluding the audience that they are watching events in real time really comes into its own in well-directed dance sequences.

CHAPTER

8 Directing techniques

Comedy

The director's most important function is to appear confident about the strength of the script. This is true of any type of dramatic direction but it is particularly true of comedy. This can be difficult enough if the comedy is being played by talented actors but when you have one or more star comedians in the cast it becomes even more difficult. Comedians, as a dangerous generalization, are creatures of mood and often very insecure. If you are in a trade where you are considered to be as funny as your last show and it is evident that you have somehow been saddled with a script that is as funny as a mad cow at a Sunday school picnic then tensions are sure to rise.

The script for a feature film comedy is likely to have spent a great deal of time in development and is less likely to suffer from the problems of uncertainty that more frequently beset television comedies. Lack of time, money and the constant need to think of something new for next week all assert their various pressures. It can be hard to judge a piece of visual comedy from the written page and we have all seen less than wonderful scripts rescued by the comic charisma of the leading players.

So how does the director best approach the world of comedy which, like German humour, is seldom a laughing matter? Strangely, some of the best advice is very basic indeed. People's reactions to a situation are usually more funny than the situations themselves. Seeing the health inspector eat the suspect veal is reasonably funny – watching Basil Fawlty's reactions as he looks on helplessly is a great deal funnier. So is the technical direction of comedy all about close-ups and reaction shots? Well, 90 per cent of the time, yes it is! A comic line played in a wide shot will never get as big a laugh as when it is played in close-up, and the effect is usually better if we cut to the close-up for the punch line. The danger is that to film those necessary details, which maximize the laugh, takes time. This is when comedians get edgy and bored. The joke seems less and less funny at every new set-up so the compliant director is tempted to cut corners and end up with an unsatisfactory edit.

Comedians are used to hearing audiences laugh at them and when there is no audience they are uncertain of the strength of the material. It is then that the director needs to engage maximum diplomacy. He should also engage a supportive crew. Lively professionals are what is wanted and preferably no 'comics manqués' and also no miserable bastards. (These two categories are best absent from any crew.) The director of comedy often has to decide on how much embellishment to allow to the script. I have worked on scripts which were so goddam awful that they were 'gagged up' by the star, the director, the first and second assistant director and the designer in order to get any laughs at all. At the broad end of the spectrum this is just about allowable but such methods are unlikely to win awards. Even when you are working with good scripts you will still need to inject comedy business to keep the film bubbling along and, again, suggestions may come from any member of the crew. It is for the director to decide what to include and what to reject, and this needs to be done tactfully. Don't be too proud to accept a suggestion and always have the grace to acknowledge whose idea it was – you never know when you might need another.

The good director of comedy has a clear vision as to what type of comedy he is directing and invents comic business accordingly. It might get a laugh if you ask Lady Bracknell to trip and fall face-first in the cucumber sandwiches but the wit and balance of 'The Importance of Being Earnest' are unlikely to benefit from such antics. However, if French and Saunders were doing a pastiche 'classic serial' then something as broad as being catapulted into the tea trolley could be hysterically funny, especially if it was timed to come after a passage of 'Merchant-Ivory style' preciously polite small talk.

The director of comedy should adapt his style in the same way that the composer of incidental music would supply a very different type of music for a production of 'Three Men in a Boat' than he would for 'The Alternative Comedy Experience'. There are, of course, grey areas whereby business that works perfectly well for one production, with one set of actors, is too much for another production of the same play. Take 'Billy Liar', for example. In the scene where a desperate Billy is spiking the frigid Barbara's drink with passion pills, the screen offers the director a better chance for some fun than does the stage.

Let us say that Barbara and Billy are sitting on the sofa and, after enough rejection, Billy gets up and comes forward to the sideboard on which he has the port 'to celebrate' and his concealed passion pills. The camera can see Barbara on the sofa over Billy's shoulder.

The essential detail for the audience to see is that Billy is putting 'passion pills' into Barbara's drink. In the deep two-shot described above we will certainly be able to see Billy's action and as he has his back to Barbara he can hide what he is up to; but we need additional close-ups to get the best out of the situation. First, we need a close-up of the bottle (clearly labelled 'passion pills') as Billy undoes it and pops a pill into Barbara's drink. We need this shot in order to know that it is sex he is after – otherwise he might just be trying to drug her. If you think 'passion pills' is a somewhat unsubtle label then think of something else; perhaps an Eros and a big heart, but it must be clear to understand as it will only be on the screen for a few moments. Now this is the point at which additional comic business is possible; just how much is a matter of judgement between director and cast. After putting the pill in Barbara's drink Billy turns towards her. This would be a close-up of Billy from Barbara's point of view. Then we cut to a single of Barbara from Billy's POV. She is looking extremely unsexy. Billy quickly turns back and pops another pill into her drink before rejoining her. This additional business will get a chuckle. You could raise the stakes by repeating the process. Billy turns again, Barbara looks even less sexy so he turns and empties the whole bottle in. This would get a big laugh but honestly is it real? Might it not kill her? There is no right or wrong answer. It is a matter for the director to decide, but as I write this it occurs to me that a better idea, one that will get a laugh and also be true to Billy's character, is that when he turns back the second time he leaves Barbara's drink as it is but takes a couple of the pills himself.

The best comedy has its feet in reality. Why 'Fawlty Towers' was so funny was that there were always good logical reasons why Basil's behaviour was so extreme. We, the audience, knew and understood his behaviour but the other characters in the hotel didn't share our knowledge and to them he seemed as mad as a hatter. 'Fawlty Towers' was a fine example of comedy construction, the lunatic situations always developed logically out of believable circumstances.

The best comic business obeys the same rule. Deciding that a character should have an irritating laugh or wear a ridiculous hat is hardly the acme of comic invention, but if these actions are seen to be increasingly aggravating to a downtrodden husband or embarrassed teenage daughter, they could be amusing. The director needs to consider if the humour is external (for the audience only) or internal (achieving its humour from the reactions of other characters within the film). As a very general rule, external humour will be less subtle and more suited to farce and slapstick. If we return to the example of the woman wearing the ridiculous hat then we can quickly see that if the actress simply appears looking ridiculous this will achieve an 'external' laugh but if the wearing of the hat embarrasses her husband this will 'internalize' the comedy and, I believe, make it funnier still.

Any stage business must grow out of the relationship between the characters; the difference between business in a horror film or a thriller is that in those genres you certainly don't want laughs but in comedy you do. Laughter is a natural release and there is a distinct danger that horror films can stimulate unwanted laughter. If a horror film requires the vampire to drink a goblet of blood a wise director would request a silver goblet. If the 'blood' is in a glass it will be much too reminiscent of tomato juice (which it probably is anyway). The thought that it must be tomato juice could prompt an unwanted giggle. If the same scene occurs in a comedy vampire 'send-up' then the blood could well be in a glass and the vampire might be directed to add a dash of Worcestershire sauce before he swallows it.

A great deal of comedy is built around the unexpected. 'Man walks down street towards banana skin, steps over the skin and falls down an open manhole'. Classic silent movie or 'Tom and Jerry' stuff. You can make use of the unexpected in comedy business. Imagine a scene with Fred and Jack having a tea break. Fred is making the tea and, unseen by Jack, he puts a huge amount of sugar into Jack's mug. Jack takes the mug and sips the tea. He doesn't like it. That will get a minor laugh – a bigger laugh will be achieved if Jack sips the tea, doesn't like it and then adds more sugar.

Delaying the comic information will often provide the best effect. I recently directed a corporate training video which featured the imaginary career of the firm's eccentric. The script called for the character to live in a house that was definitely the odd one out in his street. The production manager found a superb location. In a row of suburban 1950s semis, someone has turned theirs into a country cottage. It looked so bizarre as to be hysterical. It was just what the script called for. The house looked 'funny' by itself but the full humour was its incongruity. The audience needed to appreciate this. I therefore decided that the best way to reveal the house was to see a postman coming up the street, thus establishing the suburban normality. He approached camera and we panned with him as he delivered a letter to the 'cottage'. This treatment maximized the effect. It established the street and delayed the reveal. The odd house looked all the more out of context on film because the establishing shot delayed its 'reveal'.

The screen's comic greats certainly knew the value of the unexpected. Oliver Hardy is about to cue off in billiards. We expect him to rip the cloth but in fact his cue breaks the glass in the cabinet behind him. It is very possible to build this 'comedy of the unexpected' into the business you devise for the characters in a scene. The drunk comes home and tries to get upstairs as quietly as possible only to knock over something and wake up the whole house. Try not to make it the most obvious thing that he knocks over. Anticipation is a strong ingredient of comedy so let's say that as the drunk enters the hallway he nearly knocks over a vase. He manages to save the vase, turns and nearly knocks over the hall stand but saves that as well. However, as he turns to go upstairs we see that his long scarf has caught on one of the hooks of the hall stand. He starts to climb the stairs, takes a couple of steps, there is a huge crash as the stand falls over. A routine such as this obeys the comic rule of three which, for some almost magical reason, always seems to enhance the comic effect.

Business such as that described above is certainly elaborate. The script may simply read 'Bill returns home drunk and wakes up the whole house'. The point is that if the piece is a comedy then it is the director's job to see that Bill wakes up the house in as funny a way as possible, always bearing in mind the style of the piece itself. There is comic business to be had out of a character's anxiety resulting in events that are exactly the opposite of what they intended. Colonel Brisket goes to wipe a speck from his immaculate dress shirt only to leave a huge mark from the sponge he was using. Claude is so anxious to be correct at the tea table that he spills milk all over Mrs Fothering-Smythe, etc. A director needs to assess his cast carefully because, if he has not worked with them before, there will be some who are better at comic business than others. For one version of 'The Importance of Being Earnest' that I directed I hit on the idea that everyone in the first-act tea party was so anxious to be polite that they kept passing on the full cups of tea as they were handed them. As a result Lady Bracknell always ended up with two cups. No sooner had she put one down than she received another. This eventually worked well but took a deal of rehearsing which involved five of the cast. Some of them were better at comic business than others and I decided that I was glad this was a film version as I think the same business on-stage might have ended in disaster.

Simultaneous action

Comedy often requires the director to bring action to the screen, action which is sometimes complicated in the extreme. Here is an example.

Scene: pub interior
Fred turns suddenly and jogs the arm of the man who is about to throw a dart. The dart flies out of the man's hand at an obtuse angle and hits Bert, who is about to pot a ball on the pool table, in the backside. Bert's cue rips the cloth – the ball spins through the air and hits the cuckoo clock on the wall. The cuckoo flies out on the end of a

broken spring. The clock falls to the ground hitting Mavis on the head. The cuckoo lands beak-first in the bull's eye of the dartboard.

Action like this requires a clear storyboard/shot list and will take a deal of time to execute. In any cause-and-effect sequence it is vital to establish the relationship of the various elements before the sequence starts. For example, you might start the scene on the cuckoo clock and pan down to see Mavis underneath the clock. Fred then leaves the bar and crosses the shot; the camera pans with him to reveal a cat asleep on a chair, Bert playing pool and the darts match taking place behind him. The cat is not mentioned in the original stage direction – but it will provide us with a useful comic cutaway later. Now we have established where everyone is in the pub the use of close-ups is the most practical way to show the various inter-dependent disasters. For example:

Mid-shot: Man about to throw the dart, Fred enters shot.
Barmaid: 'Fred you forgot your crisps!'
Fred turns and jogs the dart player's arm. (Notice that we've added a line from the barmaid to motivate Fred's sudden turn.)
The dart flies out of the man's hand.

This action might well be visible in the mid-shot. However, you might play safe and take a close-up of the dart leaving the hand. You will also be sensible to use a 'safe' dart, one with no point on it.

The next shot in the sequence will be a close-up of the dart hitting Bert in the backside. Reverse motion is the easiest way to achieve this. The dart is fixed into a piece of cork in the actor's trousers. On action the dart is pulled out using an invisible piece of fish line. The shot is them printed backwards. The next shot is the close-up of the cue ripping the cloth and the ball leaving frame. Close-ups at this point will not only simplify the action, they will also allow the substitution of the real baize for a fake piece of pool table – saving the genuine cloth and allowing for retakes.

The ball flying through the air will be difficult and could be helped by a close-up of the barmaid turning her head as she follows its path.

Next is a close-up of the ball hitting the clock and the clock falling off the wall. The original script says the cuckoo flies out on the end of a broken spring as the clock falls to the ground, hitting Mavis on the head. Just as we adapted the script by the addition of the barmaid's line so I would suggest a slight alteration here. The cuckoo flying out and the clock falling are two separate actions which split our attention and we are in danger of 'defying real time' in the final gag when the cuckoo hits the dartboard. I suggest that it is better for the cuckoo to fly out as the clock hits Mavis on the head. This keeps a clear delineation between the various actions. This sequence will obviously require several special props and a lightweight cuckoo clock is one of them. As the cuckoo flies out a cutaway of the cat following its travel will get a laugh. Waving a titbit just out of shot will achieve the action you will require from the cat though you might well need to speed up the shot.

Finally, a close-up of the bird hitting the bull's eye is easily achieved using the same reverse action we employed for Bert's dart. The thing to remember about reverse action is that the cuckoo is pulled out of the dartboard but because the shot is printed backwards it appears to fly into it. The pull wire is therefore at the opposite side of the shot from that which the audience expects.

These are the basic shots to achieve the effects required from the script but there are some extras that will help with the comedy. The first point is to consider that the chaos really comes out of nothing. It would be better if we added some shots before the first wide shot in which Fred crosses with his drink. If the sequence ran:

Wide shot – bar, close-up – Bert concentrating on his pool shot.
Close-up – darts player throwing first dart and concentrating hard.
Close-up – Bert again, he decides to employ a cue rest.
Then the wide shot as Fred crosses.

This will have built a tension so the comic release will seem all the funnier.

The second detail we could polish is the use of our cutaways following the flight of the ball and the bird. At the moment we have only two: barmaid follows the flight of the billiard ball, cat follows the flight of the cuckoo. Remember the rule of three! If there was another similar cutaway before the cat, then the cat would become cutaway three and be all the funnier. I would therefore suggest a cutaway reaction of Fred as the clock falls from the wall. Even within a complicated piece of slapstick the rules of comic construction can still help to maximize the comic effect.

Action sequences

The storyboarding and trickery involved in the sequence described above indicate that comedy and action sequences have a lot in common. It is true that the complexities of photographic trickery and the paraphernalia of the stuntman's equipment (air bags, jerk harnesses, pneumatic rams, firesuits, etc.), all part and parcel of any action-packed feature film, are not encountered every day by the average sitcom director. Even so there are basic do's and don'ts for bringing convincing action to the screen and no self-respecting director should be ignorant of them.

Take the most simple action imaginable – a man running. This could be for a chase or a comic knockabout. It might be part of a dream sequence. Whatever its purpose the director has a choice of options open to him. Does he need to exaggerate the man's pace for dramatic or comic effect? Should the man appear to be running hard but getting nowhere, as in a dream? A straightforward choice of camera height and lens type will immediately invest the action with a specific 'feel'.

For example, if our actor runs towards a low camera and that camera is fitted with a *wide-angle lens* he will appear to be running faster than he actually is. If he runs towards an eye-level telephoto lens he will appear to be running hard but getting nowhere.

The more powerful the telephoto (the longer the focal length), the more dream-like the sequence will appear to be. We have discussed the effects of lenses on speed earlier but they are particularly important when directing action. A punch towards a wide-angle lens with the camera up close will look fearsome. These are practical examples of the effects of lenses in the summary of the cinematography section but, to continue in the practical vein, let's reiterate that if our man/horse/car drives across the scene photographed by a wide-angle lens the action appears slower. If this same lateral action is photographed by a telephoto lens it will seem much faster than it really is. It is perfectly possible to shoot a car travelling at a safe speed and by use of the lens alone make it seem to be travelling like a bat out of hell. Therefore the first questions that any director should ask himself before starting any action sequence are: 'am I using the best lens?' and 'is the camera at the best height?' Altering the apparent speed of action by a simple choice of lens has the advantage that the movements still look natural. This is less likely to be the case if the director chooses the other method of altering the speed of the action.

Undercranking and overcranking

In the early days of the cinema the film was driven through the camera mechanism by the cameraman turning a crank handle. It was quickly discovered that if the cameraman turned the handle slowly (if he undercranked) the action when projected seemed faster. If he turned the handle faster (overcranked) the action appeared to be slowed down. The effect is easily explained when one considers that the speed of the projected film was constant. If the film went through the camera at 5 frames per second and the projector showed it at 16 FPS then obviously the action seemed faster. If the camera overcranked to 32 FPS then shown at 16 FPS it would seem twice as slow. Sixteen frames per second was the standard speed for silent movies. When sound came in the frame speed was increased to 24 FPS as this allowed for better optical sound quality. Nowadays 24 FPS is standard for cinema films. TV films in countries with 50-cycle mains (like the UK) shoot TV movies at 25 FPS. This is simply because the process of scanning the film frame for broadcast is much easier if the frame speed synchs up with AC main cycles (2 × 25 = 50). When feature films (shot at 24 FPS) are shown on British TV they are run at 25 FPS and therefore run faster. This isn't really noticeable, yet perversely if you show a film shot at 25 FPS at 24 FPS it seems to be taking place in treacle. An awful dead hand seems to come over the whole film. This happened to me at a press viewing once so I speak from bitter experience. Always make sure that the viewing theatre can run at both 24 and 25 FPS.

What this also reveals is just how careful you need to be when changing the speed by under- or overcranking. If you are going for an obvious effect (Keystone Cops or dream sequences) then the actual degree of under- or overcranking can be pretty arbitrary. Seventy frames per second will look dream-like and 75 FPS will look almost the same. However, if you require an effect which will be unnoticed by the audience you must be much more careful. Undercrank by 2 FPS (from 24 to 22) and it will enhance the pace of a fight; one frame more and the screen heroics could tip over the edge into bathos. As an example of this effect look at action sequences from classic Hollywood swashbucklers when they are on TV. Errol Flynn's sword fights photographed at 22 FPS for cinema projection at 24 FPS look great on the big screen projected at the proper speed but on television at 25 FPS they have a whiff of farce about them.

Nowadays the speed of action on video can be changed at the post-production stage so you can gauge the correct amount as you edit. If you are working on film it is best to shoot a test before committing a whole sequence to too much undercrank. Remember that, while slow motion is available on video, film is the only medium which actually obtains more picture information when shooting slow motion – 75 pictures per second instead of 25. That is why it looks so smooth. Video slow motion merely slows up the delivery of the original picture information; the equivalent of shooting at 25 FPS and showing each frame three times.

Fights

Any decent-looking fight will contain a number of stunts and a host of deceptive camera angles to make punches look as if they are connected or to conceal stunt boxes, etc. A screen minute of fast action could well take a day to shoot. Nowadays the choreography of the fight is left to the fight arranger so the filming of a fight sequence is rather like shooting a pre-choreographed dance sequence. The director should still be sufficiently involved in the fight arranging to make sure that those involved stay true to their characters and that the fight matches the style of the rest of the film. The fantasy chandelier-swinging stunts of 'Sons of the Musketeers' may look out of place coming at the end of 'Hamlet'. The more athletic parts of the fight will be best performed by stunt doubles and you should use doubles as much as possible. The point worth remembering is that stunt artists get well paid simply because their knowledge and expertise is such that they are the least likely to be hurt. It is a good idea if the stunt man is the same build as the actor for whom he is to double. However, if the switch from actor to stunt man double is achieved on a slick action cut and the stunt starts hard on that action cut it is amazing what you can get away with. One stunt man, Stuart Fell, regularly doubled for both Ronnie Corbett and Ronnie Barker. He points out that simply falling through frame, it really isn't noticed if he is 5 ft 3 in. or 6 ft.

Doubling stunts for the small screen of TV are more easily achieved than for the cinema where a big screen enables easy comparisons between actor and double. Either medium benefits from striking costumes (period or modern) which catch the eye and thus help the deception of the switch from actor to double. If the colours are striking the eye will focus on the costume rather than who is wearing it. An experienced stunt man will always turn his face away from camera as much as possible when doubling. Construct your sequence so that it is possible to cut to the stunt hard on the action. Imagine that you have the hero fighting a stunt man over a fast-running river and the fight concludes with the stunt man falling into the river. It would be unwise to cover such action in one shot. If the initial fight looks a bit feeble this is what will register with the audience no matter how spectacular the fall may be. There is every likelihood that the stunt man will 'prepare' just before the fall and this makes things look false. For example, if he is to fall from the bridge as the result of a punch he will have to get his bottom over the railings. It is therefore helpful to break down the sequence into a minimum of two shots, dividing the sequence at the start point of the fall. Such coverage will ensure that:

- There can be as many takes as possible of the fight without involving the fall
- It is possible to edit out the preparation
- It is possible to edit the best version of the fight onto the best version of the fall
- There is much less chance of injury as the stunt man only has to think of one stunt at a time
- The fight and fall can each be shot from the most suitable angle

● Should the stunt man be doubling for an actor then the fall will *have* to be filmed as a separate shot. In such a case shoot the fall first and then match the preceding fight to it. It is much easier and safer to choreograph the fight to suit the start point of the stunt than to ask the stunt man to perform his fall from a predetermined position on the bridge with a predetermined body position to match.

All the major drama schools have combat as part of the curriculum, so a trained actor should have some knowledge of sword play and unarmed combat. It goes without saying that some actors will have learned more than others in this area of their craft and some may have forgotten what they learned and need a refresher course.

There is the age-old danger that when asked 'can you ride?' or 'can you fence?' any actor will instantly say 'yes'. He may not be lying, but his idea of riding could simply be the ability to gallop a horse and not fall off; cast as a cavalry officer he will still look less convincing.

The director should therefore be particularly careful when casting an action-packed drama. A fencing foil available at the audition is very useful. Simply ask the actor to pick up the foil and make a few passes – you will quickly be able to judge if he really can look convincing with a sword. If 'he can ride' ask him when he last rode. If the answer is 'last weekend' then he probably can ride, if it is 'five years ago' you may need to reconsider.

Film action has one great advantage over stage action – it can be broken down into easily memorized chunks. If the hero and villain have rehearsed a few short routines, these can be incorporated quite simply into any fight that the script requires. If the location and images change, then the audience will not notice that the sword play is a repeat of the same basic moves.

Filming with animals

Filming with animals is one of the many taxing problems that will sooner or later come the way of an action director. Like any taxing problem, the way to deal with it is to find the simplest and most convenient answer and, like so many things in film making, this does not necessarily mean the cheapest answer.

For example, stunt horses are available and are just as important as stunt riders. The temptation to book nags from the local riding school simply because they are cheap should be avoided like the plague. No actor, even if he is a good horseman, will appear impressive on a creature that looks as though its next canter will be in the general direction of the knacker's yard. A recent television series made this mistake *in excelsis*. Not only did the production book riding-school hacks, they believed the extras who told them they could ride. The predictable result was that on 'Action' some of the horse troop supposedly accompanying the king's coach remained stationary, some galloped off at a tangent and three or four riders succeeded in emerging from the forest backwards. The lesson is simple – if you need horses to look like cavalry, then book the cavalry. It will be expensive – you will have to pay the regiment a fee and each trooper full Equity rate – but you won't waste time and you and, more importantly, your audience will not be disappointed.

The fulfilment of audience expectation is the key to any good action sequence. Generally, horses do not rear up and pound off at the gallop, but it looks good if they do. Horses that perform this and other numerous film stunts are available and even horses have docile doubles, so a nervous actor does not have to worry about controlling a spirited stallion as well as remembering his lines.

Persuading horses to fall as if they have been shot is always difficult. The good old days of Hollywood were bad old days for horses as some very cruel devices were used to get a horse to fall. Trip wires and the infamous running W (a wire which when jerked by the rider pulled the horse's front legs up so it fell on its knees) were frequently used to spectacular – often lethal – effect. The running W is now banned and film makers fortunately prefer to use horses which have been trained to fall.

However, it must always be remembered that for a horse to fall at the gallop is a dangerous feat. It should obviously be filmed on soft terrain and, if it is possible for the rider to fall rather than the horse, this is much more easily achieved.

Action involving horse-drawn vehicles will again require specialist advice. Some general tips may be useful. Remember that the turning circle for a coach-and-four is large. A superb-looking eighteenth-century track will provide problems if there is no convenient point at either end at which to turn the coach around.

Carriages are much more safely galloped uphill than down, so try to find a location with a slight incline up towards the camera position. Riding downhill or driving a horse-drawn vehicle downhill is difficult. If the script requires this, it is perhaps best to employ camera tilt to give the impression of a steep slope. Of course, the steepness of the hill up or down can be enhanced with this trick. Taken to extremes, if the camera is laid on its side and an actor crawls along a rocky path, he can be made to look as if he is climbing up a steep cliff – many a Dracula has ascended the walls of his castle using this easy illusion.

With the possible exception of highly trained horses and dogs, animals are generally unpredictable and sequences involving them are unlikely to be one continuing delight. In BBC Television's programme

'The Scottish Tragedy' two important animals were involved. One was a toy poodle, the other a falcon. Endless problems were anticipated with the vicious-looking bird of prey, but not with the pooch. How wrong! The falcon behaved impeccably, flying and landing on cue, remaining quiet when required to do so. The poodle, however, yapped continuously (except when the recordist wanted to record a wild track of the yaps, then it went into the canine version of a cataleptic trance). In fact, generally, it behaved as though Robert MacBain, the actor playing its loving owner, had mistreated it horribly as a puppy. This was not the impression required. The old adage about working with children and animals had been forgotten – if an animal is booked as 'prop', all the director can expect is that it appears on the set. Should it be required to 'perform', it should be booked on an artist's contract at a much-increased cost.

Geese and chickens, if they have a mind at all, have a mind of their own and need constant rounding up between takes, but do bear in mind how useful they can be in adding a sense of panic and confusion if they are disturbed as part of the action in a period piece. If that action takes place in a castle courtyard, it is not too difficult to control their wanderings. Obviously, only set them in at the last moment.

All animals should come with experienced handlers and their advice and requirements must be heeded. It is particularly important when creatures like chimps are on the set – chimps may look adorable but can bite viciously, as many a bloodied actor can attest.

Crocodiles and reptiles obviously need experienced handlers. In my experience they tend to become lively under the heat of studio or film stage lights. One tip, therefore, is to keep them crated or boxed in a cool environment because, say zoologists, they become sleepy when their body temperature drops.

There really is no such thing as a reliably trained cat, though a number of people have made a modest fortune perpetuating the myth. When Roger Corman was filming 'The Tomb of Ligiea' a cat was required to stalk menacingly across the set and pounce at Vincent Price. After hours, some accounts say days, with the cat looking placidly at the crew as if to say 'Darlings, I can't possibly go on', a solution was found. The sequence was filmed as the cat shot across the set trying to escape a jet of compressed air aimed at its rear. It was the unfortunate Mr Price who suffered the humiliated animal's revenge.

Directors are well advised to avoid the use of the word 'Action' on any scenes involving experienced film animals when such animals are required to stand still. Horses, in particular, soon learn to move off as soon as they hear 'Action' so if your shot requires the carriage and pair to stand still while the highwayman talks to the occupants of the coach, it would be better to say 'Cue the dialogue' instead of 'Action'.

Breakaway props

The director should always bear in mind the fact that balsa wood is not the easiest material to work with and so furniture made from it is usually rather primitive in design. Medieval furniture can be easily mocked up in a breakaway form but an eighteenth-century dining chair would probably take longer to make in balsa wood than it took Chippendale to make in walnut. In such a case, it would be better to smash a vase. Vases can be effectively made in wax and painted to look genuinely valuable.

Wax bottles and vases are much the cheapest of the breakaway props. Glass objects, such as transparent bottles and window panes, are made from a plastic resin whose manufacture is stringently controlled by health regulations. Props made from this material look very real but are expensive. If you are planning a large scale 'punch-up' (a pub brawl or so on), it is always worth while to ask visual effects if they have any breakaway props left over from a previous production before committing yourself to what can turn out to be a very costly property bill.

The visual effects designer is responsible for any **pyrotechnics** required (explosives, bullet near-misses, etc.). In such cases he will certainly be on the location and will require a recce to determine his cable runs to the various charges and to decide how to hide both cables and charges. It is a great help if you can be precise about location and intended shot size. Remember that explosions take a while to set and reset. The effect of machine-gun strafing will involve many charges as it is, in fact, not one effect but a series of linked effects. Make sure that artists and camera crew are well versed in the sequence of the charges. Resetting a strafing effect really does take time.

Bullet hits

For bullet hits on people, the visual effects designer will place a small charge in a contraceptive and fill it with stage blood or offal. The actor wears a lightweight metal breastplate under his shirt and the charges are attached to this plate. On detonation, a bloody hole is blown in the shirt.

The actor needs to be fairly static for this effect to be easily accomplished. It would be impractical for him to be running in a wide shot while trailing yards of detonation cable.

So what if we want a running man to be hit by a bullet in a long shot, and we want to make use of a bullet-hit effect as part of the sequence? Such problems can waste hours on location, unless we apply a little tangential thought. For example, our running man could be stopped, or at least slowed down, by a bullet in the wide shot (by simple acting) and then be killed by a second bullet in a closer set-up (for which we employ the bullet-hit effect). Such compromises to practicality can save vast amounts of time on location and, if the audience cannot identify compromise in the finished sequence, nothing has been lost at all.

Compressed air jets are often employed for supernatural effect (pages turned, etc.). It is easy to forget that a strong compressed air jet can be very dangerous indeed and so, again, the effects designer has the ultimate say in how such devices may be used. It is possible for the most dangerous stunt or spectacular explosion to look unimpressive on-screen if the shot has been badly directed. The same rules about lens choice and camera height that we saw in relation to the 'running man' apply to stunts and visual effects. In other words, just because experts are on hand, there is no excuse for the director to sit back and leave it all to them.

Fire scenes

Fire scenes are much less terrifying to execute than might be generally supposed. The visual effects department will be very much involved and an FX team of three or four operatives under the direction of the visual effects designer will be required.

The flames themselves are most commonly generated by **flame forks**. These are flexible pieces of piping fed by a small cylinder of Calor gas. The flame forks are dressed in place for each shot to give maximum effect. A flame fork underneath the lens is always a good idea with a second fork at a safe distance behind the actors. The combination of smoke and a long-focus lens to compress the shot will bring the flames to within an apparently dangerous proximity to the artists.

If flame forks are used with due regard to the visual effects designer's advice no actual damage should occur to the set. However, it is probably best to use such devices on a set rather than in a real location interior.

If time is not at a premium and you really want things to look spectacularly dangerous, it is worth considering the use of a 60/40 mirror. Placed in front of the camera lens the camera 'sees' the action through the glass of the mirror, but the mirror also reflects flames from a fire fork positioned beside the camera. The use of such a device (an adaptation of the front projection process) can place the actors right inside the flames.

There is bound to be a degree of tension and excitement on the set at the outset of any action sequence and this is particularly true of fire scenes. To avoid accidents there are a number of important rules.

It goes without saying that all safety regulations should be obeyed and all specialist advice heeded but, in addition, the wise director will allow sufficient time for a full and complete rehearsal of each shot before the flame forks are lit. After 'light-up' a run through at half-speed will ensure that everything is safe and also allow the cameraman to check that the flames are in the optimum position. (The foreground flame forks can sometimes blot out too much of the action and have to be adjusted accordingly.) It cannot be emphasized too strongly that one of the most important contributions a director can bring to the safe completion of a potentially dangerous shot is to ensure that everybody on the set knows exactly what is going to happen and what is expected of them.

If the sequence requires an artist's clothing to be on fire then you will certainly need the services of a stunt man. Fire suits with breathing apparatus covered by rubber face masks are available for human torch effects, but the fee demanded for such stunts is commensurate with the risks involved.

For exterior fire scenes – buildings on fire and the like – it is possible to conceal flame forks near the windows of a building and achieve a convincing result. The visual impact will be much greater if the sequence can be filmed at night. It might even be advisable to change the time of a fire in the script to night-time if at all possible.

Some really spectacular footage has been achieved by employing a lot of flame forks in the windows of already ruined buildings – again using the veil of the night to disguise the truth that the buildings are already in disrepair.

Finally, the director should consider that showing the start of a fire can present a problem. It is difficult, time consuming and expensive to show the fire gradually taking hold of the room, so an oil lamp falling over and setting fire to curtains will also be better than a candle (period permitting). If the time-scale of the sequence requires a period of time to elapse before the fire is seen in its full fury, then construct the sequence in such a way that you can cut away from the original ignition. For example:

1 Cigarette butt smouldering on saloon carpet
2 Hotel guest getting into bed
3 Saloon carpet bursts into flame
4 Hotel guest sits up and smells burning
5 Hotel guest descends stairs
6 Smoke coming from under saloon door
7 Hotel guest (unwisely) opens the door to reveal the saloon in a blazing inferno.

Smoke

The important point to remember (if budget is a prime consideration) is that to see a fire start and spread, you actually have to set objects alight, but a blazing inferno can be convincingly achieved using smoke and flame forks, thus causing no actual damage to set and dressings. One of the most useful adjuncts to an action scene is smoke. In the battle scene of Orson Welles' masterly film 'The Chimes at Midnight' smoke was one of many clever devices used to disguise the small number of extras involved. A pedant might argue that a medieval battle would be pretty low on smoke as gunpowder was not yet in general use. However, Welles' subtle introduction of it looks completely believable. Certainly an eighteenth-century battle will appear all the more effective for the inclusion of smoke and, again, the television director could use it to disguise the real number of soldiers involved in the production.

Smoke can be generated in a number of ways. If a power supply is available, then the smoke gun is probably the best method. A smoke gun works by passing two gases over a hot element and the result is dense, white smoke which is controllable and reasonably inoffensive. The gun requires about 10 minutes to warm up, so try to remember to give notice that you intend to use smoke three or four slates in advance.

Larger, but still portable, smoke guns are available for exterior use. They use Calor gas instead of an electric element and can provide volumes of smoke. On a still day, two such units can fill a small valley area with convincing 'mist'.

Pyrotechnic smoke candles of the type used on army exercises are available. They can give white smoke, black smoke, indeed a range of colours, but once started, they cannot be extinguished and the density and quality of smoke produced makes them unsuitable for anything other than exterior use.

Dry ice (that is, solid carbon dioxide) produces a dense, white mist when dropped into water. Dry ice machines are available with ducting to pump this mist about the set as required. Two things to remember about dry ice are:

1 It is heavy and lays about the set, usually settling approximately one foot from the floor
2 It is a mist, i.e. droplets of water, and therefore everything gets wet. This is important to know if you have a painted studio floor. It will quickly reduce the floor paint to a slippery, dangerous mess. The use of dry ice in a dance sequence, for example, can be very dangerous (oil spills on the floor from the older type of smoke guns can give similar trouble). If you plan to use dry ice in a

sequence that involves dancing or fast action, the best solution is not to paint the floor at all ... after all, it won't be seen anyway.

The use of smoke to give a dusty or sleazy atmosphere to a bar set or a romantic feel to the stables at dawn is always very effective and the lighting effects possible with a little smoke in the atmosphere to act as a trigger are numerous and exciting. One word of warning – scenes using smoke absorb time. It is very difficult to get the smoke to a similar density on every shot and this can only be achieved by putting in a lot of smoke before each take and turning over only when it has cleared to the right density.

In the section on lenses, it was pointed out how useful the foreshortening effect of a long-focus lens can be in making objects seem closer than they are in reality. Do bear in mind that a mild pantomime flash can be made to look like a devastating explosion if it appears to go off close to the camera or close to an artist. The safe distance is about 8 feet but the lens can reduce this real distance dramatically. It is sometimes helpful to edit in one flash frame (i.e. clear film) at the start of a small pyrotechnic effect. The same trick, combined with appropriate sound effects, can also produce reasonably convincing lightning.

Lightning

Lightning can be created either at the post-production stage or on the set using special lighting equipment. In post-production over-exposing a couple of frames can produce a convincing effect if combined with the appropriate sound effects. On the set small areas can be supplied with lightning from a light source fitted with shutters (a sort of giant Aldis lamp). Large areas require that you hire a device such as a 'lightning strike' which discharges a huge amount of light on cue and is much safer than the old DC scissor arcs.

Action locations

Any film buff will immediately recognize the street 'lot' which Warner Brothers built in bricks and mortar in the 1930s. The intersection, with the subway on the corner and the typical Bronx houses, has appeared in countless films and is still frequently used, especially when the script calls for a traffic accident in a busy street.

Car crashes, bank raids, riots, etc. are in themselves difficult enough but the problems for any television director in finding a real location for such incidents are obviously enormous. If a studio street lot is available (and it is always worth checking to see if any of the big studios have anything still extant from a recent production) then it is almost certain that a false geography will have to be created. In other words, while the get-away car is filmed speeding through a genuine built-up area, the actual collision where the car crashes, overturns or bursts into flames is filmed in a different, private, location. This two-part solution to the problem still needs detailed planning to prevent it ending in disaster.

First, police permission and co-operation must be sought just to achieve the shots of the car speeding through the town. The police cannot condone the breaking of a law, such as the speed limit, for a film and will probably insist that it is shot early on a Sunday morning – which is not much use if the street has to look busy. In this case, it would be best to plan the scene in such a way that most of the carving through the traffic is done as a car interior (using a camera mounted to the car or perhaps having the vehicle on a low loader). The advantage of interior shots is that they easily exaggerate speed and if you have some other cars under your control travelling fairly slowly in front and behind the principal vehicle, they will add to the illusion that the getaway car is travelling fast.

Exterior shots in such a sequence will prove difficult especially if the writer wants a car chase through central London. In that case, a telephoto lens following specific vehicles across the axis of the screen could be a simple, effective solution. The police forces of big cities are generally anxious to discourage filming and it takes a combination of tact and determination to obtain the permission required. However, always get this permission and always stick to the restrictions imposed.

If the script writer has been more practical and merely asked for a chase through an unspecified town, life is much simpler. Some small towns will be amazingly co-operative and may even close a couple of streets for an afternoon. Seaside towns out of high season can be very helpful, especially if the town council can be persuaded that there is some publicity to be gained. It would therefore be possible to start the chase sequence in central London, using the devices described above, and then stage the collision in a seaside town.

Some training colleges and redbrick universities have roadways on their campus sites that look very much like ordinary roads and, again, these are worth considering for any car-chase sequences, especially out of term time. In the 1970s, when motorways were springing up all over the country, it was often possible to find a stretch of roadway which was nearly complete but not yet officially opened. This is less likely nowadays, but again an enquiry to the Ministry of Transport could still pay off.

The question of period locations is really unanswerable as every script will call for different requirements. The designer will therefore be a vital member of the location-finding team. In particular, he will be able to advise whether an unwanted piece of modernity can easily be disguised or if it is possible to supply a missing monastery on the hill or the mountain range behind the castle by use of glass shots or electronic paint-box effects.

It will be a tremendous help if the writer of a period series is familiar with the chosen location. His skill can then be used to turn necessity into advantage and he is less likely to pen story ideas that are really impractical to achieve within the constraints that the location has imposed on the production. Most stately homes and ancient monuments in the care of the Department of the Environment are very dependent on the revenue they receive from visitors, so they will require a considerable fee to close down for a period while you film. If work can progress around the visitors, the fee will be much less, but the frustrations considerably greater; if it is possible to afford it, have the place to yourself. It can often be advantageous to film some interior scenes on location at the great house and mix these with interiors built to match on the sound stage. This will probably be an absolute requirement if any heavy action (swinging on chandeliers, etc.) is involved.

Chases

The rules of screen geography apply as much to chases as they do to battle or fight scenes – though, of course, in a chase the pursuer and the pursued must always be seen travelling in the same direction across the screen (either left to right or right to left). Again, the power of editing can be illustrated by considering the implication of the order in which the images appear on the screen. If the first image the audience sees is of a bull charging left to right across the frame and then the editor cuts to a shot of a man running left to right the statement of visual grammar is that the man is chasing the bull. As logic would tell us that this is unlikely to be the case, such a presentation may cause some confusion but the audience will most likely 'work out for themselves' that the bull is, in fact, supposedly chasing the man (unless the man is dressed as a toreador). If the characters in the chase are less obvious stereotypes, then the audience will take the visual information at its face value and therefore the director must be punctilious in his attention to screen grammar.

Imagine a fairly well-worked action scene – members of the French Resistance are driving their Citroen LT 15 furiously across country (left to right) and the Germans are pursuing them in a Mercedes. A sudden cut to either vehicle going right to left could have a catastrophic effect on the structure of the chase. If the change of direction was first seen in a shot of the Citroen, the implications would be that the Resistance had decided on a collision as their only hope of escape. A cut to the Mercedes travelling right to left would imply that the Germans had given up and were heading for home! This is yet another case where 'cut and dried' theory is all very well but the actual practice can be a minefield for the unwary director.

On location some good shots may be unobtainable unless the vehicles are travelling in the opposite direction to that which has been generally established. The direction of the sun might force the cameraman's hand or the need to exclude anachronisms from the background may mean that for some shots the vehicles have to travel right or left. The rules are therefore obvious; when recceing locations for a chase, establish the direction which works best for most of the sequence and, if some shots have to be done with the vehicles travelling in the opposite direction, then remember to shoot some footage in which the leading car changes direction. In fact, a planned change of direction can enhance a chase, but the audience need to be clear in their minds about what is happening. A safe approach would be to have several shots of each car driving straight to camera and ensure that they leave frame left in one take and frame right in another.

Shots in which the participants in a chase exit frame from the same side as they entered are also very useful to bridge over a change in direction. Such shots are not difficult to achieve. It is often possible to find a stretch of road that snakes across country and position the camera in such a way that the vehicles enter frame-left, drive down the road towards the camera, and then *exit left* on a bend.

Chase sequence example

Wartime vehicles, especially Mercedes staff cars, are very scarce indeed so nowadays even large budgeted feature films find it imprudent actually to write off historic vehicles. The following specimen shot list is compiled with due regard to the need to simulate damage to the vehicles involved.

Script:
LUCIEN AND FRANÇOIS DRIVE THEIR STOLEN LT 15 CITROEN THROUGH A ROADBLOCK. THE GERMANS GIVE CHASE WITH A MERCEDES CAR AND TWO MOTORCYCLES. FRANÇOIS MANAGES TO KILL ONE OF THE MOTORCYCLISTS BUT EVENTUALLY LUCIEN LOSES CONTROL OF THE CAR AND CRASHES INTO A TREE.

Shot list:

 1 The German roadblock. Guards stand around rather bored. The motorbikes are unmanned, the Mercedes staff car is parked and faces back up the road. (Facing away from the direction of the eventual chase. This will allow sufficient time for business in turning around when the chase starts and give the Resistance a believable 'start'.)

 2 Lucien and François driving along (camera either on a side mount or shot against front projection).

 3 CU Licien, as he sees the roadblock ahead.

 4 Roadblock as seen through the windscreen. (It would be a good idea to film at least one version of the crash through the barrier from this angle and intercut it with the exterior 'crash through'.)

 5 German guards rushing to the barrier preparing to fire their machine pistols, etc.

 6 BCU Lucien's foot, hard down on the throttle.

 7 Through windscreen again. Germans in front of the barrier firing. (Undercrank and perhaps zoom into a guard as he is knocked out of the way.)

 8 Exterior (low camera and wide-angle lens): the car crashes through the (balsawood) roadblock. (If a dummy soldier is set on the bonnet at the start of the shot this can effectively cut with 7. Bullet hit (visual FX) on car detonated from inside the vehicle. (It is worth noting that if planning to use the dummy soldier trick it would be well to shoot an alternative version in case the dummy looked fake on film.)

 9 Empty frame: the Citroen drives in from behind camera and goes fast up the road. (Again, low camera angle and wide-angle lens.)

10 The Germans rush to the bikes and start them up, the Mercedes starts and swings around stirring up dust, etc.

11 Cut-ins for above BCU-kickstarts, etc.

12 WS with recognizable landmark (windmill?), the Citroen driven across frame left to right.

13 2S: Lucien and François – Lucien looks at the fuel gauge.

14 MCU: fuel gauge nearly empty.

15 WS with windmill: the motorbikes followed by the Mercedes cross frame left to right. (The landmark will give the audience a reference point to estimate how close the Germans are. If more shots between 11 and 14 are included, then the distance will seem greater.)

16 François throws a grenade out of the Citroen window.

17 BCU: grenade lands on the road.

18 Motorbikes approach camera, pull focus to grenade big in foreground – visual FX explosion to wipe out frame with smoke and flash.

19 BCU: injured motorcyclist rolls into frame.

20 MCU: German fires out of the Mercedes.
21 Lucien is hit in the shoulder.
22 Citroen swerves down road fast to camera, exits past camera left pursued by the Mercedes.
23 2S: Lucien slumped over the wheel, François looks up horrified.
24 View through the windscreen as the car veers off the road towards a large tree (undercrank).
25 Shot with tree 'foreground': Citroen enters frame-right and hits the tree (undercrank and reverse motion). The car is parked up by the tree with one set of front wheels up on a wheel ramp. This tilts the car over and the ramp is masked from the camera by the tree. If the car is reversed away from the tree the shot printed backwards will give the impression that the car not only hit the tree but also rose up as it did so. It is necessary then to cut away quickly on impact so the next shot is ...
26 BCU: François knocked unconscious as he jerks forward.
27 The Mercedes approaches camera: pan as it stops by the wrecked Citroen. (It is easy to surround the Citroen with smoke and fit fake smashed panels to give the impression of considerable damage.)

The example above has expanded a short piece of script into twenty-seven shots and approximately one-and-a-half days' filming. It must be noted that all the shots of Lucien and François in the Citroen (shots 2, 3, 6, 12, 15, 20, 23) and the shot of the German Officer (shot 19) could be achieved by the use of a camera mounted to the side of the car but they would be much more easily achieved as a process shot (front projection, travelling matt or on electronic camera with CSO).

Editing action

Editing is perhaps the most creative single task in any form of film making and, in action sequences in particular, the ability of the editor to create cause and effect is of paramount importance. A battle sequence may contain many shots of archers loosing arrows and soldiers dying with arrows in them. If the editor cuts from one of the archer shots to one of the 'dying soldier' shots the audience will believe that the archer has shot the soldier – if the shots are put together the other way round (the soldier first, then the archer) the audience assumes that the soldier has been shot by an unseen hand and the archer is shooting at someone else. The director need not have too finite a plan when he actually films the battle but he must realize that he needs plenty of shots of archers and plenty of shots of soldiers (with and without arrows in them) for the editor to decide who kills whom.

What the director can do, irrespective of whether action involves longbows, crossbows, pistols or rifles, is to get the maximum number of 'shots' from each set-up. An actor aiming his arrow can be shot from the side with the arrow pointing out of frame left. The cameraman can easily zoom in and take a big close-up of the arrow point. He can also get a big close-up of the archer's face. Turn the archer through 45 degrees and there is a shot looking along the arrow towards the target. Turn him through 90 degrees and there is another archer firing in the opposite direction. With advice from the armourer and the arrow not actually in contact with the bowstring, it would also be possible to take a shot of the arrow aimed straight at the camera. All this from one camera set-up!

A golden rule of any battle (gun-fight or chase) is that if one army is marching from left to right the opposing army must approach from right to left. Blindingly obvious? Maybe so, but compare the battle scenes in Laurence Olivier's films 'Henry V' and 'Richard III'. In 'Henry V' the rule is obeyed, indeed exploited to the full and in 'Richard III' it is almost completely ignored. As a result 'Henry V' contains one of the most memorable screen battles ever filmed, while the battle scene in 'Richard III' is disappointing. It is perhaps interesting to note that in the sequence where Richard's horse gets shot, Sir Laurence decided to abandon visual effects and editing trickery and employ an Olympic archer to fire a real arrow at his charger. The horse was protected with padding and light armour under its caparison. Unfortunately, the archer missed and the arrow penetrated Sir Laurence's costume armour, pinning him to the saddle. A close-up of an archer firing, cutting to a whip pan, cutting to a shot of the arrow in the horse, would have been much easier to achieve, a lot safer and, arguably, just as effective. As the hail of arrows firing into the French knights in 'Henry V' was a simple optical, it would be fascinating to know what persuaded Sir Laurence to abandon trickery for such dangerous reality in his second battle.

Stanley Kubrick's battle scenes in 'Spartacus' and 'Barry Lyndon' are brilliant examples of sequences in which the director wishes the audience to appreciate the tactics of the battle and, at the opposite end of the spectrum, Orson Welles' battle scene in 'The Chimes at Midnight' is a brilliant montage of picture and sound which places the audience in the heat of the conflict. Different though their styles may be, both directors obey the left-to-right rule. Welles, with his need to stretch limited resources (250 extras on a very wide screen) perforce employed every editing trick at his considerable command. On analysis the knight who gets hit by the mace and chain is not the same knight who falls off his horse, but this is only revealed after many reruns of the sequence. The fact that there is a hard action cut from a shot of one knight hitting another to a shot of a knight falling to the ground is sufficiently convincing. The loud crash in the sound track at the cut point completes the illusion. Much of the violence of Welles' battle is conveyed by the sound track – the image of the dying horse (wounded by yet another arrow) is all the more distressing because of the whinnying on the track.

Action Summary

- Provide as many 'cut-ins' as possible for any fight. This will help to cover up any disappointing action and allow the editor to change takes if necessary.
- Devise parallel action whenever possible. If the editor can cut from the fight to a fuse burning or the cavalry on its way to the rescue, this will increase excitement and provide a seemingly legitimate reason for cutting away from the fight. The actual reason may simply be that the fight looked fake after that point, but no-one will realize this if the action we cut to is exciting and relevant to the sequence. It is worth noting that the fuse burning is more exciting than the cavalry galloping to the rescue, as the fuse represents imminent danger but the cavalry, imminent relief. In other words, one cutaway builds more tension than the other. Should the cavalry get ambushed, then the 'frustration factor' will bring the tension to a still greater peak. The worst cutaway of all for a fight is the heroine watching helplessly – this does not build tension unless the lady picks up a handy pitchfork and joins in!
- One of the most useful shots in any sword fight is a close-up of each swordsman 'fighting the camera'. When you take these shots try to ensure that the background is in really soft focus. This will enable the editor to cut close at any point without too much regard to the geography of the wide shot.
- Remember that editing can cheat speed. If you cut from a shot of the hero about to draw his gun to the baddy going for his gun and we hear the hero's gunfire before we cut back to the hero with a smoking pistol in his hand, it is the editor who has made our hero the fastest gun in the West.
- Remember that in any confrontation (armies marching towards each other, gunmen advancing down the street, etc.) the film editor will cut the shots shorter and shorter to build the tension. Help him by planning the images so that they get more and more imposing as the sequence progresses.
- If you are really stuck in the cutting room with some shots that are unconvincing, do not forget the post-production's ability to speed shots up – enlarge them, tilt them or even reverse them left to right.

The director's role

I think that 'role' is exactly the right word to describe the director's job as there is a deal of play-acting required if you are ever to be truly successful. It is important to be able to appear confident when you are not; contrite when you are sure you are in the right; angry when you are not really and jolly when you are in fact bloody furious. The good director knows exactly when to indulge in the right permutation of the various deceptions, the bad director does not. The one thing a director should never appear to be is arrogant. The process of film making is much too collaborative and co-operative for one person to be foolish enough to suppose that he always knows best. Actors and crews alike know this and, while they will put up with a great deal from directors whom they respect, arrogance in a director ferments contempt. A contemptuous cast and crew can drop the director right in it. The ability to be honest with yourself is a vital attribute for any director. Decide the real worth of the project both for you and the production for whom you are working. If it is your first job on a long-running soap opera then all that is required from you is to deliver a professional-looking show on time and on budget.

Attempts to demonstrate a unique visual style will be as unwelcome as they are foolish. If you have been chosen to direct a one-off film for TV then a more individual style may well be welcome but make sure you have the producer, the director of photography and the star(s) 'on-side' before you start shooting. If the film is your project and you have struggled to raise the money, buy the book rights or write the script, find the cast, etc., etc. – then you have every right to make the film exactly the way you want to. That will not mean that you are immune from star tantrums or logistic location nightmares so try to allow some time between clinching the finance and starting the shooting – otherwise you will not have sufficient energy to give of your best. The few people I know who have had the guts and determination to raise the money to make their own feature films have all said that raising the money was such a nightmare they almost lost sight of the original enthusiasm they felt for the project.

Enthusiasm is the key. Actors need to feel that the director has confidence in the project. 'All right then, folks, let's knock this old rubbish on the head' may be a disarmingly honest approach but not one that is likely to inspire much commitment from the cast. It is worth remembering that everyone on the set has a private life which may be going well or badly and that everybody has their own secret professional insecurities. It is all too easy for the first-time director to believe that he is the only one on the set with problems; that everyone is against him or that no-one is taking it seriously. In the cutthroat world of freelance film making it is very unlikely that the unit is not taking it seriously. It may well be that to preserve themselves from a nervous breakdown they are making light of difficulties. If you have an honest working relationship with your cast and principal crew members the shoot should proceed smoothly enough. Sometimes, however, an 'atmosphere' can develop and you may not be sure why.

The three people on the film who really know what is going on are the star's dresser, the make-up artists and the sound recordist, in that order. The reason is obvious when you think about it. The dresser gets to hear all the star's moans and dislikes, the make-up artists hear all the gossip as the actors stumble into make-up for their early-morning call and the recordist often hears choice pieces of private conversation picked up on the microphone between takes. Incidentally, make-up artists have an important role as therapists to nervous actors as they prepare them for the day's filming. Actors like to relax and feel cosseted in the make-up caravan. The wise director does not venture into make-up with a vast array of notes as this will be perceived as an invasion.

Orson Welles once experienced that inexplicable 'atmosphere' on set when he was directing Edward G. Robinson in the film 'The Stranger' (1946). Something was upsetting Edward G. and Orson did not know what it was. He was sensible enough to ask Edward G. Robinson's dresser. 'Well, you see, Mr Welles,' he said 'you're con-tinuously photographing Mr Robinson from his bad side.' 'Oh, I see,' said Orson wisely, not confessing that he did not realize that Edward G. had a good side.

A director should never be dismissive of an actor's need for direc-tion. 'Just get off the bus and walk into that shop' is not much of a direction, especially to an actor who has just arrived on the set. Even if the action is simply part of background movement performed by an extra it will look much better if you say 'So this is a cheerful scene and we're using your action as you get off the bus to bring the camera round on to Emma and Hugh. Imagine you've just got engaged and are going into the shop to choose the ring.' A direction like that, which honestly does not take a whole lot of energy, will at least stimulate the right mood from an extra and get the scene off to a good start.

It is attention to details such as this which makes all the difference to the commitment that cast and crew bring to the project and that is the sort of 'plus' a director can bring to the journeyman type of direc-tion. Your episode of a soap opera is much more likely to stand out above the rest if the performances are all given at 100 per cent than if 'Coronation Street' suddenly appears to have gone 'film noir' for the night.

The pressures on the director at the time of the shoot are many and various – you can't ignore them. It is important that you keep to schedule and budget but you must switch off from them while you are actually shooting a take. It is all too easy to get into the 'after this' mode of thought. 'After this shot I must do a close-up, then all I need is three more shots and we will be out of here.' It is good to know exactly how much more you need to complete the sequence but there is a danger that you spend so much time thinking about what comes next that you fail to concentrate on what you are filming at the moment.

There is also a danger that you will never enjoy what you are doing at the time you are doing it. After all, we all of us had one hell of a struggle to get to the position of director and there is not much point if we cannot savour it. More seriously, once the director has decided on a take – that's it! There's no going back, so you need your full concentration as the shot is being filmed to be confident of your decision to 'print it'. In the 'out of time' world of single camera drama the director must have an absolute grasp of the story and the emotional development of the characters. At 8 o'clock in the morning on a freezing winter's day it is possible that the actor hasn't got the clearest idea of where this particular shot fits into the scheme of things. In such a case a note from the director that this shot comes just after Joe has had a row with Anne and just before he sees Liz for the first time could be most useful.

In fact the more that everyone on the shoot is conversant with the script, the better. Sir John Mills, when working as a director, always sent scripts to the whole unit; sparks, grips, carpenters, the lot! This is not just good PR – the director is bound to get the best work from a crew that feels involved. A director's first task is to persuade cast and crew to give of their best.

You will not get through a career in film making without there being some rows on set but the canny director can even turn those to his advantage. If an actor, even a star, is 'throwing a wobbly' the director must be quick to act. The first thing to do is to decide if there is a genuine grievance and, if there is, sort it out but the most important thing to do is to appear calm and in control. If you are obviously rattled you will be the victim of emotional bullying for the rest of the film, if not the rest of your career. If it is obvious that real complaints are swiftly dealt with but equally ego-trip screaming sessions run off you like water off a duck's back, they will quickly cease to happen. A united cast and crew will soon silence the mutterings of a potential trouble maker and the director will emerge all the stronger for calmly riding out the storm.

The situation where one star actor demands all the director's attention while other equally important actors are seemingly left to sort it out for themselves is always dangerous. Try not to be taken down that treacherous path and certainly make sure that the less demanding actors get their full share of your attention. Enquire after their close-ups, if they are happy etc. Again, tactfully handled, the situation will defuse itself but left to fester, an almighty row is brewing. Sometimes a difficult situation will resolve itself in an unexpected way.

There is a story concerning Dame Edith Evans and Dame Sybil Thorndyke. They were co-starring in a West End play and the awful decision had to be made as to which of the two grand dames should have Dressing room No. 1. Dressing room No. 2 was exactly the same size and just as convenient except that to reach the door you had to ascend one small step. The director reticently approached Dame Sybil and said 'Now, Sybil, about dressing rooms.' 'Don't worry dear man,' she said, 'I know exactly what you are going to say. Of course Edith must have Dressing room 1, she'd never manage those stairs!'

Working with the designer

The designer's (art director in the USA) job varies enormously from film to film, indeed from scene to scene. Sometimes on location it may be a simple task of laying down some rubber cobblestone mats to disguise a modern tarmac yard; sometimes the addition of a few pieces of suitable furniture to an already furnished room. More often it will involve the refurnishing, indeed redecorating, of a whole house or the construction of a number of interiors in the studio, often a mixture of both. In British television there is a division of responsibility between set designer, costume designer and make-up designer. In the USA there is more of a hierarchy, with the 'art director' very definitely at the top. This is probably a better system as a co-ordinated look should not be left to chance. In the UK you can get some stunning results if all three designers are working as a team and some bizarre effects if they are not. It is the director's task to oversee the whole production and therefore he should 'chair' the initial meetings between design, costume and make-up. It is just as important for these three key production people to share your views about the characters in the drama as it is for the actors playing those characters. A panning shot over a bedroom to reveal the hero in bed can be much more than a device to establish the geography of the room. The curtains, furniture, pictures and ornaments can all tell as much about his lifestyle as can his pyjamas, if he is wearing any.

In the heyday of the talkies all films were studio-based. Some exteriors were on location but all interiors were built on the sound stage. Union restrictions and a quest for 'reality' persuaded more and more directors to shoot everything on location and nowadays few television film makers think of studio sets as their first option. This is a pity, especially as now few of the union difficulties still apply. The space and facilities of a studio, in my opinion, cannot be beaten. The director and the designer can work together to achieve exactly the right look for the film. It would, for example, be almost impossible to recreate the style of 'film noir' on a real location. The interiors of Xanadu in 'Citizen Kane' or of Miss Haversham's house in 'Great Expectations' are redolent of an atmosphere that is well-nigh impossible to achieve unless you are on a sound stage; in particular, that marvellous scene when Pip pulls down the curtains and lets the sunlight flood in. Remember the problem of contrast we discussed earlier if we were using real sunlight. Set construction and the hire of studio space is unquestionably expensive but the long-term hire of a real location is by no means cheap, and all I would do is to suggest that the director at least considers the possibility of shooting on the sound stage; it really will give a much greater deal of creative freedom to the designer and there are ways to keep the cost down.

The actor, Richard Todd, once told me how cost-conscious Walt Disney used to be when it came to the production of his historical live action dramas. A studio so versed in the production of cartoon features saw no reason to build a foot more scenery than was actually necessary. Each director was required to storyboard the film in such detail that for every scene the bare minimum of scenery was constructed – no chance to decide on the shoot that you needed an unplanned wide shot. If the agreed storyboard showed a close-up that is all the backing that would have been constructed. This might well have been rather too draconian, but it is a good example of just how economic the designer and director, working closely together, can be.

Props

Personally I love props and if I arrive on the set to find a wonderful period gramophone or radio I will often try to include it in the action. This is a rather unprofessional confession because, of course, props should be divided into two categories: action props (which are used by the actors) and dressing props (which aren't). A gun that the actor picks up is an action prop – a gun on the wall is a dressing prop. Even so, the task of prop buying (more usually hiring) is a chancy business. Sometimes there is a gem of a dressing prop, sometimes not. When there is it seems a pity to me not to see it gets a good outing.

Sometimes in a period piece, the director has to take a decision about the suitability of a prop. Some designers really will worry if the phone is *circa* 1905 and the play is set in 1890. This may be important if you are making the definitive biography of Alexander Graham Bell but not really if you are making the average 'House of Horror' gothic movie. It is worth noting that our telephone would be no cause for concern at all if the dates were reversed – if the play was set in 1905 and the phone was *circa* 1890. This general point is well worth noting. Most domestic interiors at any period have a lot of furniture and ornaments from previous decades. Only the executive's *office* of 1935 would be pure 1930s. His home would probably contain a good deal of inherited furniture. Again it is a design and directorial decision as to how much of the inherited furniture our executive would keep. Is he the sort of go-ahead 1930s yuppie that would chuck out Edwardian heirlooms? Again, another example of design making a character point. The director can reasonably easily disguise a poor prop on the rare occasions that one turns up on the set. The quill pen that simply will not write is pretty common as is the 'champagne' cork that won't pop. Unless these props are part of the film's climax a lot of time can be saved by simply shooting around them – close-ups of the poet's face which cut to his creation just after he has finished writing rather than during the writing process, etc.

I've mentioned the chance to feature an obvious prop like a gramophone but, of course, the camera also gives us a chance to savour more subtle props. Kath's excruciating taste in crockery as she serves Mr Sloane his breakfast for example. A close-up of the plate could establish both period and character and might even stimulate a nostalgic chuckle from those members of the audience old enough to remember when such crockery was in vogue.

Floor plans

The designer will provide the director with floor plans and furniture positions if the sets are to be constructed and on major productions will provide such plans, as are required, of the location interiors and exteriors. I have never been very bright at reading floor plans and am always grateful for a model of the set. I find models much more useful for plotting camera moves and working out if there is sufficient backing or height to avoid shoot-off. It is worth noting that television scenery is usually constructed using flattage that is 8 ft tall whereas feature film sets usually use 12 ft as the standard. This is important if you are considering using low angles. The camera does not have to drop much below eye level before you shoot off an 8 ft flat. Television adopted 8 ft as a standard simply to ease the fast turnround that was needed in the days when TV drama studios were in use seven days a week. If you are working with 8 ft flats and you really need a low shot the answer is to use ceiling pieces. These can cover the back corners of the set and allow for realistic-looking low angles. If these ceiling pieces do not intrude too far into the body of the set they can be left permanently in place without compromising the lighting.

There are many things to check as you go through the set plans with your designer. Shoot-off is probably top of the list. Which way the doors open is important too. Does one wall have to be especially strong (because someone gets thrown against it)? Are important pieces of furniture 'gettable' for the camera? Is there sufficient distance between the windows and the backing cloth for the view to look sufficiently diffused so as to appear real? Equally, is there enough room for backing cloth lights? Often the director can help a design problem by some simple business.

Some years ago I was working on a small-budget horror movie and was lucky enough to have Oliver Bayldon as my designer. Oliver had constructed a wonderful Gothic staircase with a huge window at the half-landing. For reasons of economy we were in a smallish studio and, through no fault of Oliver's, when the camera was at the foot of the stairs looking towards the window you could see the top of the skycloth cyclorama. Adjustment would have been costly in both materials and time and we had already shot half the scene with the camera on the landing. At this angle the 'sunset' through the window looked wonderful. It only looked fake when we wanted to cut to the low angle as the young squire moved off downstairs. I am almost ashamed to admit that for ten minutes we panicked a bit until I thought of the blindingly simple solution. It was this! Just as we cut wide I directed actor Nigel Descombes, playing Stopes the butler, to step forward and draw the curtains. It was all perfectly logical. He was the butler and it was getting on for dusk and, most important of all, it hid the shoot-off!

Another trick we used on that film was to have a small section of corridor built and by re-dressing it gave the impression of endless rambling passages (see Figure 8.1). Sara Coward and Nigel Descombes walked down the corridor towards camera position A passing the door on their right. We then re-dressed the set and moved the camera to position B. The two actors then entered frame and walked towards the door through which this time they went. On-screen it looks entirely convincing. The bedroom that they entered was also used as two separate rooms in the film simply by refurnishing it and altering the principal camera position.

I have mentioned doors already but equally important is which way cupboard doors open. Nothing is worse than finding that the cupboard door opens towards camera thus neatly masking everything inside it. Breakfast scenes can be a nightmare as faces get hidden behind props. The greatest offender is the large packet of cornflakes. This is a pity, because cornflakes are easy to eat and

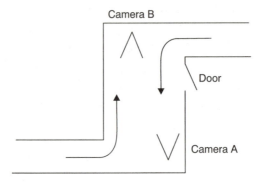

Figure 8.1 Re-dressing the set.

much more kind to the actors than bacon and eggs. The solution is to use those variety packs of mini-size packets. Cornflakes packets may seem an odd thing to mention in a section on design but remember, it is the design department that supplies them and you get what you ask for.

The difference in height between the head of someone standing talking to someone sitting often forces the camera to widen more than is ideal. The design department will usually have blocks called 'two four sixes' which can raise the chair, table, etc. by 2–6 inches, thus solving the problem of height differential and don't worry, it is a device that goes unnoticed.

Mirrors

Unless you intend to use a mirror for a reflection shot then it is best not to have one on the set. If there is a mirror on the set you will find it irresistible. Mirrors can be a blessing as they allow us to see both faces in an over-the-shoulder two-shot.

If you are planning mirror shots make sure you have a good-sized mirror (3 ft × 2 ft). This will allow you to contain a good deal of action within the frame. Mirror shots require a deal of rehearsal to make sure you don't see any equipment (especially the camera) in the reflection. It is sometimes difficult for the actors to find a suitable eyeline when you are shooting into a mirror as the angles used to exclude the camera falsify reality. The director needs to be patient and explain the problem to the artist. It is one of the rare occasions when it might be helpful for the actor to see the shot in the viewing monitor. If you are shooting into a mirror make sure to include at least some of the frame, otherwise the edited shot may not appear to be in a mirror at all and merely look left-to-right reversal (see Figure 8.2).

Figure 8.2 Mirror shot.

You can have great fun with mirrors. I remember a shot we did in 'The Importance of Being Earnest'. Quite by chance my camera operator, Les Newsome, realized that the position of Lady Bracknell and Jack allowed him to shoot flat on to the mirror. In most circumstances this would have given a large-as-life reflection of the camera. It just so happened that Lady Bracknell's body masked that part of the mirror so we obtained the apparently impossible.

Mirrors, as dressing on the set, are best avoided as the danger of unwanted reflections (especially of the boom) is just not worth the risk. Glass on the set in cabinet doors and picture frames is also best avoided if possible as lights are all too easily reflected. Glass doors are the worst, as they are almost guaranteed to reflect all the lights as they swing open or closed. Sometimes you have to live with a mirror if you are working on location and it is fixed to the wall. Large mirrors in stately homes are often screwed to the wall and it is risky to remove them. The design department might consider supplying a picture which fits within the existing frame and transforms the mirror into an oil painting.

As long as the mirror is not featured too much in shot, painting over the glass with neat washing-up liquid will blur the reflection without harming the mirror itself.

1 Exercise scripts

When I was producing the drama element of the film direction courses at BBC Television Training it became quickly evident that there was a shortage of interesting scripts that could be sensibly attempted with only half a day's rehearsal and one short day's filming. I decided the best recourse was to write some myself.

I include ten such scripts in this final section which the student film maker is free to use for non-broadcast exercise purposes. None of the scripts are without their various technical demands and they are arranged in ascending order of dramatic and cinematic difficulty.

Notes for 'Moments to Go'

The following direction notes for the script 'Moments to Go' may well prove useful as a general catalyst to your thoughts as you direct both this and the other scripts in the set.

1 Is Luke a skinhead? Is he black, Asian? How old is he – 16, 20?
2 As Luke runs up the stairs towards camera a long-focus lens would help the sense of panic and otherworldliness.
3 As Luke enters the 'safe haven' of the office would it be good if there was a pause before Iris speaks? In other words Luke notices her only when she speaks.
4 Iris – what social type is she, how is she dressed? Is she on tranquillizers and, if so, how much has this affected her speech and demeanour?
5 Iris: 'I don't want you here, get out!' Does Iris stand here or is there a better time to stand later on in the piece?
6 Luke: 'Is he still here then?' Is Luke momentarily frightened by the thought that Dr Mackenzie might still be around?
7 Iris: 'Dr Mackenzie says I was suffering from stress but I'm better now. Much better than I was' (some heavy gun-fire on the sound

track)*'Oh my God it's getting worse' (*although there is no mention of it in the script this is surely a good place for Iris to stand).

8   Luke: 'Here have some of this.' This is Luke's first indication that he has some sympathy for Iris. The fact that his offer is refused results in the next section of the dialogue being argumentative. The scene should not be static at this point as it needs to feel 'settled' later on. Luke could idly go round the office seeing what's worth stealing while Iris, seated once more, views him with disdain.

9   When Iris starts to cry we have another chance to see that Luke is really soft-hearted. He can cross and get closer to her than before. As he offers the bottle he could cross in front of Iris and settle on the other side of her. A left-to-right change of screen positions at this point will provide a subtle indication of the change in their relationship. This section can be covered in a close two-shot and two close-ups.

10 Luke: 'It's gone quiet outside.' A reminder that there should have been a lot of riot sounds from the street up to this point and that the actors will have needed to pitch their performances accordingly. It would be effective, if slightly time consuming, to take a shot of Luke looking out of the window from an exterior camera position between the lines 'It's gone quiet outside' and 'do you think that means?'

11 Luke: 'Oh God I'm scared.' Iris: 'You shouldn't drink like that.' Luke is by the window – this is an opportunity for Iris to move to him and perhaps take the bottle from him. Luke could move into the middle of the room on the line 'What's the time?' Iris joins him on 'I never did see Swan Lake.'

12 There should be a pause after Luke's line 'but it ain't the same is it?' before we hear the 'threatening drone'. Then if Luke moves back towards the window for 'I dunno, must be the bomber or the missile or whatever the bloody thing is.' This will give him a distance to travel back to Iris on her line 'Hold on to me Luke, please!'

13 'It's quiet in here, we're safe in here.' Definitely a close-up but after that a high shot of two little people alone in the room would be very effective; even more effective would be a crane up as the sound increases – perhaps a mix to 'burn out white' rather than a fade to black would be appropriate.

14 It would be best if the windows were covered. Venetian blinds would be ideal. This will exclude distracting reality and also allow for low-key lighting through the scene.

1 'The Power'
       by

  Mike Crisp

****

THE OFFICES OF NIGHT LIFE MAGAZINE -
DARREN HAS HIS FEET ON THE DESK AND IS IDLY
THINKING THROUGH SOME PAPERS. DARREN IS
ABOUT 30 AND IS THE OFFICE BULLY. HE IS
PROBABLY SO UNPLEASANT BECAUSE HE IS
SPECTACULARLY BAD AT HIS JOB. EARL, A YOUNG
COLOURED GUY AND THE OFFICE JUNIOR ENTERS -
BRINGING DARREN HIS LUNCH - A TAKEAWAY COFFEE
AND A BURGER (OR WHATEVER)

<u>EARL</u>: There we are, one coffee with, and one
Jumbo Burger heavy on the onions easy on the
ketchup.
  (DARREN TAKES A BITE)

<u>DARREN</u>: It's cold.

<u>EARL</u>: Well of course it's cold. The takeaway's
two streets away.

DARREN: You are a lazy little bugger, do you
know that? Next time you get my lunch you run
back with it, understand? Run.

EARL: Oh yes boss, 'course boss, sure thing boss.

DARREN: I should shut it if I were you -
remember what happened to Jane.

EARL: She's got a better job now anyway.

DARREN: Well, she's white isn't she?

  (EARL LOOKS AT DARREN WITH REAL HATRED BUT
   SAYS NOTHING. EARL CROSSES TO HIS DESK AND
   NOTICES IT IS PILED WITH PAPER WORK.)

EARL: What the hell's all this?

DARREN: A bit of overtime for you - chance
to earn enough to buy a bigger ghetto blaster. OK?

EARL: Fine - only this time I'm claiming all the
overtime.

DARREN: Oh no matey. Miss Harmen thinks we
share the work and that's the way it's going to
stay.

EARL: Tell me one thing will you, Darren -
answer one simple question?

DARREN: Depends what it is?

EARL: Why are you such a prize shit?

DARREN: Oh Earl, I've upset you, forgive me,
I had a wretched childhood, my father was eaten
by cannibals - probably one of your bleedin'
uncles. (DARREN GRABS HIM) I'm a shit Earl,
because I enjoy being a shit. Life's a jungle,
I'd 've thought you knew that seeing as you
were living in one so recently.

EARL: You shouldn't have said that Darren, you've
made me really angry and when I'm angry I ....
   (HE STARTS TO GO INTO CONVULSIONS)
Oh **n**o, no, no, etc. (HE SCREAMS AND FALLS ONTO
THE DESK. HE STARTS TO ROLL AROUND AS IF IN A
TRANCE)

DARREN: My God he's flipped. Here, Earl, you daft
little sod, stop it. (DARREN SHAKES HIM BUT IS
REALLY QUITE FRIGHTENED) Stop it will you!

EARL: I can see   it's started - the spirits
have come - they've come for Jane.

DARREN: Are you on a trip or what?

EARL: Jane - the great spirit has - Jane! ...

(THE PHONE RINGS, DARREN ANSWERS)

DARREN: Hello, Night Life Magazine, (EARL GROANS.
DARREN COVERS THE PHONE WITH HIS HAND)
Shut it will you? Shut up. (HE SPEAKS BACK
INTO THE PHONE) Yes, Earl works here but he
'er can't come to the phone at the moment -
what - oh oh yes, yes, I'll tell him.

EARL: (COMING OUT OF HIS 'TRANCE')

DARREN: That was Jane's mother - Jane's been
rushed to hospital with a raging fever - she
said she's sorry she ever doubted you.

EARL: Oh God. I'm frightened Darren, I don't
know what to do - it's the power, I've got the
power.

DARREN: What?

EARL: Well, the other day Jane and I were
mucking about with some of our family relics -
my grandad was a witch doctor you see and ...

DARREN: Oh yeah?

EARL: Doesn't matter if you believe me or not,
you'll know soon enough. It's the power, I can
feel it now - Oh God, Darren - we put a curse
on you.

DARREN: Well, your grandad must have been
as useless as you are - it's Jane whose got the
jitters.

EARL: That's just a release of her terrestial
spirit - No, we put the curse on you.

DARREN: Bollocks!

EARL: (HE STARTS TO SHAKE AGAIN) It was a
curse of blood .

DARREN: Is that bad?

EARL: The worst.
   (DARREN GOES TO LEAVE)
Are you OK?

DARREN: (SLIGHTLY RATTLED) Course I am, I'm going for a drink.

   (EXIT DARREN - EARL WAITS A FEW MOMENTS
    THEN MAKES A PHONE CALL)

EARL: Hello, hello Jane - Yes, you timed it perfectly but he probably won't really believe it all until the permanganate works - permanganate I put some in his coffee. No it won't harm him - it's just when he has a pee it'll be purple. Grandad's idea - he's a biologist.

   (A SCREAM OF MORTAL TERROR FROM DARREN)
Oh, I think it's worked, Jane.

****

<u>ABRIDGED VERSION</u>

2 '<u>INMATES</u>'

by

<u>Mike Crisp</u>

> (THE GOVERNOR'S GARDEN OF
> A BORSTAL. ALAN TOMKINS,
> ONE OF THE INMATES, IS
> WORKING IN THE GARDEN.
> IN THE DISTANCE, WE CAN
> HEAR PARADE GROUND DRILL
> (FX. DISC). ALAN IS
> DRESSED IN INSTITUTIONAL
> DENIM. HE SEEMS REASONABLY
> CONTENTED. AROUND HIM ARE
> VARIOUS GARDEN TOOLS.
> A LARGE PAIR OF BOOTS ENTER
> FRAME. THEY BELONG TO
> STEVE PRENTICE, ANOTHER INMATE,
> MORE AGGRESSIVE THAN ALAN -
> MAYBE STEVE HAS A REGIONAL
> ACCENT.

<u>STEVE</u>: Mr Keale reckoned you'd be slacking.

<u>ALAN:</u> So?

STEVE: He said if you were, I could
give you a good kicking N Q A.

ALAN: N Q A?

STEVE: (VERY THREATENING) No
questions asked.

> (ALAN WAVES TO SOMEONE
> WHO IS A LONG WAY OUT OF
> SHOT)

STEVE: What are you at?

ALAN: I'm waving to the Governor.
He's watching us from his office.
(FIRMLY) You see, Prentice, this
is the Governor's garden and as
long as I get the work done he
doesn't care how long it takes me.

STEVE: You're a spineless little bugger
aren't you? That's what gets up
Mr Keele's nose.

ALAN: That sod's had it in for me
since he got here.

STEVE: Well, you don't ever stand
up for yourself. Always being shoved
around, kicked by the bully boys,
slapped by the screws - you don't
ever hit back or nothing.

ALAN: So what?

STEVE: It brings out the worst in
people, that's what. Any rate you
get right up Mr Keale's nose.

ALAN: At least I only get up his
nose.

STEVE: What did you say.

   (GRABS AT ALAN)

ALAN: Oh nothing - look, why don't
you go and have a smoke ?

STEVE: A smoke? You got some **ciggies**
         then?

ALAN : Yeah.(HE PULLS OUT SOME VERY
'HOME-MADE' ROLL UPS FROM HIS BREAST
POCKET) If you go behind that tree
they can't see you from the main block.
Now leave us alone,OK?

    (STEVE MOVES OFF BEHIND THE TREE.
    ALAN CARRIES ON WORKING)

STEVE : (BEHIND THE TREE) No one is
about there?

ALAN : No.

STEVE : What about the Governor?

ALAN : He's not watching us any more.

STEVE : If you've set me up I'll......

ALAN : Look,if you don't want a smoke
stop sodding about and give me some help.

STEVE : I'm just being careful that's
all. I'm doing alright for once, I
don't want to blow it.

ALAN : Don't kid yourself. Keale won't
do you any good. He'll just use you to
do his dirty work for him.

    (STEVE LIGHTS UP THE CIGARETTE AND
    CHOKES AMID MUCH SMOKE)

STEVE: Christ, what the fuck do you
make these out of?

ALAN: Herbs, what else?

    (STEVE EMERGES FROM BEHIND
    THE TREE AND COMES UP TO
    ALAN)

STEVE: Tobacco, that's what else,
you tosser. Do you really smoke
this muck?

ALAN: Course I do.

STEVE: No wonder you're bonkers.

    (PAUSE)

And you're wrong about Keale and
all. He can get me an early parole
as long as I keep my nose clean.

ALAN: Going to give you a diploma
and all is he?   There's 3½ million people
unemployed out there, Sunshine, so where
does that put you? Right at the bottom
of the shit heap.

STEVE: I'll get a job.

ALAN : Oh yeah, grovelling to some
other bastard like Keale - that'll be
a real achievement.

STEVE : Well, any **rate**, you're being
shifted off gardening, that's for
sure.

ALAN : Says who?

STEVE : Keale of course.

ALAN : If he tries that the Governor'll
have him by the nuts.

STEVE : How come?

ALAN : I'm one of the Governor's
success stories don't you realise
that? I get paraded every time
there's a Home Office visit (MIMIC**KING**),
'and this is young Tomkins, I expect
you remember the case, very difficult
lad, simply wouldn't respond - but I
didn't give up. We'll try him in the
garden I said - and just look at the
result, magnificent!' Same thing every
year - pathetic old fart. He'll not
have me _moved_ as long as he can boast
about me.

STEVE : Boast about you!

ALAN: I'm the <u>Governor's</u> success,
don't you see? He needs me to prove
he's not a failure - they're all
failures: Keale, the Governor, all
of them - that's why they work here.

STEVE: But they're the bosses.

ALAN: Listen, mate. I've worked
out one thing. They're here because
they're failures and we're here
because the world's a bloody failure -
now give a hand for God's sake.

> (AFTER A PAUSE, STEVE
> STARTS TO HELP ALAN
> GET THE SEEDLINGS PLANTED)

3 'THE GREAT DAY'

by

Mike Crisp

(CYRIL'S CAR, RATHER ANCIENT, PULLS UP OUTSIDE
AUNTIE'S HOUSE. AUNTIE IS RUSHING DOWN THE
GARDEN PATH CARRYING A LARGE GIFT—WRAPPED
WEDDING PRESENT AND ON TOP OF THIS IS BALANCED
ANOTHER PRESENT - WE CAN HARDLY SEE AUNTIE)

AUNTIE: Come on Cyril, give me a hand.

CYRIL: Can't.

AUNTIE: I'll drop them in a minute, give me a
hand, you lazy little tyke.

CYRIL: If the engine stops it'll never start
again - I've got to keep revving it up.

AUNTIE: If I drop this present you'll never
start again.

(CYRIL, DRESSED IN AN ILL—FITTING MORNING
SUIT, GETS OUT OF THE CAR)

CYRIL: Don't say I didn't warn you.(HE TAKES THE PRESENT FROM AUNTIE) You get in and keep revving the engine. I'll put these in the boot.

(CYRIL GOES TO THE BOOT, AUNTIE GOES TO THE DRIVER'S DOOR)

AUNTIE: I've forgotten my ventilator. (SHE TURNS TOWARDS THE HOUSE)

CYRIL: Rev the car up for God's sake.

(CYRIL IS REPACKING THE BOOT AND HAVING TROUBLE FITTING ALL THE PRESENTS IN)

AUNTIE: I'm not going without my ventilator. If I have an asthma attack in the church it'll ruin everything.

CYRIL: Rev the engine you silly old woman!(HE RUSHES TO THE DRIVER'S DOOR AND GETS IN JUST AS THE CAR STOPS)

AUNTIE: Oh here it is! (LOOKING IN HER HANDBAG AND FINDING THE VENTILATOR)

CYRIL: Well that's it, then. We might as well start walking.

AUNTIE: What do you mean?

CYRIL: I told you there's something wrong with it. It won't start when it's hot.

AUNTIE: Well, there's plenty of time, let's wait till it gets cold.

CYRIL: It's a bugger to start hot or cold.

AUNTIE: It got you here.

CYRIL: I parked at the top of a hill last night specially. It'll start if you're doing 40 miles an hour. (HE TRIES TO START THE CAR) You see, it's hopeless.

AUNTIE: Where did you hire the suit from?

CYRIL: (PROUDLY) It didn't cost me a penny.

AUNTIE: I should think not - it doesn't fit.

CYRIL: (GETTING OUT OF THE CAR) I got it from my friend Jane - she works at the dry cleaners. As long as I have it back there by Monday the guy who owns it'll never know.

(CYRIL HAS WALKED ROUND TO THE FRONT OF THE CAR AND HAS OPENED THE BONNET)

AUNTIE: What are you doing?

CYRIL: I don't know - just checking to see nothing is loose. (HE MESSES ABOUT UNDER THE BONNET)

AUNTIE: You are getting that coat awfully mucky.

CYRIL: Oh damn! (HE TAKES THE COAT OFF AND HANDS IT TO AUNTIE)

AUNTIE: That lead looks dodgy to me. (SHE PULLS OUT AN HT LEAD)

CYRIL: What do you know about it?

AUNTIE: No less than you, Cyril. Here take this. (SHE GIVES HIM THE COAT BACK) Have you got a plug spanner?

CYRIL: I'll have a look in the boot.

(CYRIL GOES TO THE BOOT AND TAKES OUT THE PRESENTS - HE FINDS A PLUG SPANNER AND TAKES IT BACK TO AUNTIE)

AUNTIE: This engine is a disgrace, filthy.

CYRIL: Look Auntie, it's an engine not a bleedin' pantry.

AUNTIE: When I was a W.R.A.C. we'd've been on a fizzer if we'd let our vehicles get into this condition.

CYRIL: I didn't know you'd been a W.R.A.C.

AUNTIE: I lied about my asthma. Here, try it now.

(CYRIL GETS IN THE CAR AND STARTS IT)

CYRIL: Auntie, you're a genius.

AUNTIE: Come on then, or we'll be late.

(AUNTIE GETS IN THE CAR - CYRIL STARTS TO SING THE WEDDING MARCH. THEY DRIVE OFF, LEAVING THE PRESENTS BEHIND)

4 'AN IDEAL COUPLE'
            by
   Michael Norman

EXTERIOR. DAY.

WENDY AND MARK ARE A MIDDLE-
CLASS COUPLE IN THEIR MID-
TWENTIES. THE SETTING IS A
PLEASANT SUBURBAN GARDEN.
WENDY IS 'EDGING THE LAWN'.
MARK APPROACHES HER FROM THE
OTHER SIDE OF THE GARDEN. HE
KISSES HER ON THE NECK.

MARK: Sue says I'm to tell

you tea's in five minutes.

WENDY: Good, I should be

finished by then.

MARK: Well, for God's sake

don't be late. We don't want

any more dramas.

WENDY: Roll on Sunday

afternoon.

MARK: You hate these weekends

don't you?

WENDY: Not really. I like
the chance to do a bit of
gardening. It's just Sue's
punctuality fetish that gets
up my nose.

MARK: Tell you what, why
don't we go into town tonight
- see a film or something?

WENDY: Leave Tom and Sue
behind you mean?

MARK: That's the general
idea.

WENDY: Bit rude isn't it?
Wasn't Tom going to show us
some slides or something?

MARK: Yes.

WENDY: Well then, it's very
rude.

MARK: Yes - let's go!

WENDY LAUGHS AND WALKS OVER TO
A GARDEN SEAT AND SLUMPS
DOWN. MARK WALKS OVER TO THE
SEAT.

MARK: Shall I bring your tea

out here?

WENDY: No, I'll come in. Two

insults in one afternoon might

strain diplomatic relations.

MARK: Very likely. (HE SITS

BY HER) I sometimes wonder

how these awful weekends ever

got started.

WENDY: It was Sue's idea -

I'm her oldest friend after

all. When she married and

left London she thought a

breath of country air every

now and then would be good for

my asthma.

MARK: But you don't get

asthma.

WENDY: Not any more, not since
I became a respectable married
woman.

MARK: Not since you stopped
sharing a flat with Sue more
likely.

WENDY: True - never thought
of that. Still I don't like
upsetting Sue, so if I wheeze
down the phone every now and
then she's as happy as a clam.

MARK: She's a bit like Rabbit
really.

WENDY: Like who?

MARK: Rabbit in 'Winnie the
Pooh' - he always needed to
feel important.

WENDY: Poor old Sue's not so
bad, it's Tom who's like
Rabbit.

MARK: What, my friend Tom?

WENDY: You pretend to like him
for my sake.

MARK: Suppose I do - just as
Sue pretends to like me for
your sake.

WENDY: Let's go and get that
tea before there's another
row.

THEY RISE AND WALK TOWARDS THE
HOUSE.

MARK: Who's going to tell
them we're going out tonight?

WENDY: (PICKING UP A STONE)
Guess what hand it's in - the
loser tells them.

MARK TOUCHES HER HAND. SHE
OPENS IT AND IT IS EMPTY.

MARK: I lose - oh well - dear
Tom, I'm sure you'll
understand if Wendy and I go
into Granchester tonight.
You see Tom, Wendy suffers from
asthma, I expect Sue's told
you that. Well, it seems to
come on when she's bored so
you see, Tom, your slides could
bring on a severe attack.

WENDY LAUGHS - MARK KISSES HER.

MARK: God I love you - why
ever did you marry Tom?

WENDY: Why did you marry
Rabbit?

5 `THE PROPER AUTHORITY`

by Michael Norman

CORRIDORS   OF   ELMHURST
COMPREHENSIVE   SCHOOL.
LATE AFTERNOON - THE   SOUND OF
THE   LAST FEW   CHILDREN LEAVING
FOR   HOME CAN   BE HEARD   IN THE
DISTANCE.   JOAN   RUSHWORTH,   A
UNIFORMED   WOMAN   POLICE
INSPECTOR,   IS   IMPATIENTLY
WAITING TO   MEET   THE   SCHOOL'S
HEADMISTRESS,   BRIDGET   HARMAN.
JOAN TAKES   IN SOME   POSTERS ON
THE   WALL AND IS   MAYBE NOT TOO
PLEASED   TO   SEE   CND   AND
ANTI-APARTHEID   POSTERS   ON
DISPLAY.   BRIDGET   HARMAN
APPEARS QUIETLY   AT THE   END OF
THE   CORRIDOR AND   OBSERVES WPI
RUSHWORTH   FOR   A   MOMENT.
BRIDGET APPEARS TO   BE   A   VERY
STRAIGHT **-LACED**   SCHOOL   MARM.
JOAN   RUSHWORTH IS   BY CONTRAST
WELL MADE-UP AND 'MODERN'.)

BRIDGET   Inspector Rushworth?   So sorry to keep you waiting.   It's 'reports time', always takes an age and I didn't want to lose my train of thought.   I do hope you've been looked after.

JOAN   Oh, yes, I was given a cup of tea - half an hour ago.

BRIDGET   Oh dear, doesn't time fly? Any rate, how can I help?

JOAN   It   is   rather   a   delicate matter.   Perhaps we could go into your office?

BRIDGET   If we must.   Frankly, I'm sick of that office by this time of day.

(THEY ENTER THE OFFICE)

JOAN   Nice and quiet.

BRIDGET   The kids went hours ago and no teacher stays late nowadays.

JOAN So I understand. Well, it's about Darren Green. His parents have made a complaint against the officers who arrested him.

BRIDGET Yes, I know.

JOAN We have reason to believe that you intend to support their allegation.

BRIDGET Yes, you have.

JOAN Pardon?

BRIDGET You <u>have</u> reason to believe that I intend to support their allegation because it's true, I do.

JOAN Do you really think that that is a responsible attitude?

BRIDGET Surely it is the only attitude?

JOAN   It must have occurred to you,
Miss Harman, that in our different
ways we represent authority - the
status quo - law and order, if you
must. We have many responsibilities
but one of the most important is to
present a united front.

BRIDGET   So what would you suggest
I do?

JOAN   It might be better if you
declined the opportunity to appear
before the tribunal. You'd be
saving yourself a great deal of
trouble. This could be a very
unpleasant business.

BRIDGET   I'm not sure I understand
your use of the conditional, Miss
Rushworth. It already is a very
unpleasant business - what it <u>could</u>
be is surely for the inquiry to
decide.

JOAN   So you definitely intend to give evidence?

BRIDGET   Yes, I do.

JOAN   Even if I tell you that in our opinion there is no charge to answer? You could be accused of wasting police time. Miss Harman, what is your interest in Darren Green?

BRIDGET   I have very little interest in Darren Green, Inspector. He has been a perfect menace since he came to the school. My interest is in working towards a more civilised society. I'm not sure if Darren Green has a place in a civilised society, but I'm certain that police brutality does not.

JOAN   Old-fashioned values are very admirable, Miss Harman; unfortunately we live in a modern world. Now the charge against our two officers is a very serious one.

BRIDGET   Indeed it is.

JOAN   So, naturally, we will be putting up a very strong defence, indeed your actions will come under close scrutiny. It could be very distressing.

BRIDGET   You make it sound as if I was on trial.

JOAN   Do you actively encourage subversive activities, Miss Harman?

BRIDGET   I beg your pardon?

JOAN   Come on, you must   know the way the   wind is   blowing. Parental choice, the National   Curriculum - there is not   much   room   in   modern education for the limp and Left-wing nonsense   that   was   once   so fashionable.
(SHE CROSSES TO THE CND POSTER)
This anti-nuclear propaganda, hardly an   encouragement   to   responsible citizenship.

(PAUSE)

BRIDGET   Do you   know what   I find pathetic   about people like   you? It's   your   ludicrous   belief   that common sense   is   the   exclusive preserve   of   the   Right wing. Together   with,   of   course, partriotism, morality and   a direct input into the   mind of   God! Have you seen the state of   the books in the   school   library?   They're   all falling to bits - of   course we'll have a few raffles and a jumble sale

- maybe we'll raise enough money to buy a new set of encyclopaedias. Tell me Inspector, when did you last have to hold a raffle to buy a new panda car?

<u>JOAN</u> Well, I'd like a job like yours Miss Harman. I mean, while you're in your classroom, saving the whale, patching up the ozone layer and putting South Africa to right, Constables like the two who arrested Darren Green are risking their lives to protect society.

<u>BRIDGET</u> You <u>do</u> realise that you are seriously deranged **?** I mean, are you really so insecure that you'll forfeit every last flicker of individual thought for the security of a uniform? What are you upholding? Not the law - you break it all the time. Not the freedom of the individual - you harass anyone who stands up for their rights. It's not a society you support, it's

a club - a club of unscrupulous international profiteers with more power than you'd ever dream of.

JOAN (A TWINKLE IN HER EYE)
And is this what you'd say if we called you to give evidence?

BRIDGET Just try and stop me.

JOAN Oh, no-one will stop you Miss Harman.

BRIDGET So I will be called?

JOAN Certainly, I'll guarantee it. No, I can see myself out.

BRIDGET (TO HERSELF AS JOAN RECEDES)
Fell for it, silly bitch.

    (SHE REARRANGES HERSELF, AND ONCE AGAIN LOOKS VERY 'PROPER'.)

6 'OLD BOYS'

BY

Mike Crisp

(A QUIET ROOM AWAY FROM THE MAIN PARTY.
TWO YOUNG MEN PUSH THEIR WAY THROUGH THE
SMALL CROWD AT THE DOORWAY AND HELP THEMSELVES
TO A DRINK FROM THE GENEROUS SUPPLY OF BOTTLES
ON THE SIDEBOARD. THEY ARE GILES MERRICK (AGED
ABOUT 30) AND MARTIN HOBBS (ABOUT 23). MARTIN'S
HANDS ARE GRUBBY, PERHAPS HIS SLEEVES ARE ROLLED
UP - HE HAS BEEN OUTSIDE IN THE COLD FIXING
GILES' CAR).

GILES : My God, I'm glad that's over, it's
real brass monkeys out there - here have a
drink, you've earned it old boy.

MARTIN : Thanks, a large scotch please.

GILES : Must say, it's a real bit of luck
meeting someone who knows about Morgans -
I honestly didn't think I'd be able to drive
the old bus home - soda?

MARTIN : I'll have it neat, thank you.

GILES : Man after me own heart.

MARTIN : You having one then?

GILES : Better not - don't ask a man to
drink and drive and all that rot.

MARTIN : Can't be too careful. I reckon those brakes will be okay for a couple of hundred miles, but you really ought to get them seen to properly.

GILES : Oh I will, I promise - still can't believe my luck - it's not everyone at a party who has a full set of tools in his boot.

MARTIN : Cars are my hobby, been nuts on motors since school.

GILES : Which school?

MARTIN : Downingham, actually.

GILES : Well that explains it, I thought I knew you - frightfully sorry but I never did really catch your name.

MARTIN : Martin, Martin Hobbs.

GILES : Giles Merrick '71 - '76. I say, weren't you in my house?

MARTIN : I was a junior in Pagets in your last term. You shared a study with Ashley, I was his fag. You sure you won't have a drink?

GILES : Oh I don't suppose one will do any harm, after all this is a bit of a reunion, eh?

(HE POURS A DRINK AND RAISES HIS GLASS)

GILES : `Vivat Schola Downingensis'

(MARTIN HAS SAT DOWN TAKING A BOTTLE WITH
HIM. GILES SITS BESIDE HIM)

GILES : I say, could I possibly scrounge a
cigarette?

MARTIN : Sure, help yourself.

(GILES TAKES A CIGARETTE)

MARTIN : You thrashed me for smoking once.

GILES : Did I? Can't say I remember it but
then all the mons in Pagets were pretty
keen on thrashing.

MARTIN : Yes, you were.

GILES : 'Specially old Dog's Breath Burton.
He once thrashed some poor little sod four
times in one week.

MARTIN : Yes it was me.

GILES : Was it really? Well, I'll be damned.

(MARTIN TOPS UP GILES' GLASS)

GILES : Terrible thing about old Dog's Breath,
got blown up you know - joined the paras.
after Sandhurst and got sent out to Belfast, only
been there a week.

MARTIN : He was a sadistic bastard.

GILES : Well, yes, I suppose he was. Still,
nobody deserves that, do they

MARTIN : (TOPPING UP GILES' GLASS AGAIN)
Maybe not.

GILES : When I think about it, Pagets was a
damn unlikely house. Homewood's dead as
well, you know.

MARTIN : Don't think I remember Homewood.

GILES : Oh you must do - we called him
'Large Arse'.

MARTIN : Oh yes - I think I can recall the
face.

GILES : He was killed in a riding accident.
His old man always reckoned that some damned
hunt saboteur spooked the horse. I'd like
to meet the bastard who did it, I can tell you.

MARTIN : (POURING GILES YET ANOTHER) Hanging's
too good for 'em.

GILES : I'll drink to that.

MARTIN : What about Ashley? I think I read
somewhere that something pretty bloody happened
to him.

GILES : Oh my God, yes. He had some frightful
flat in Acton with one of those really ancient
geysers. They found him dead in the bath.

MARTIN : He was a scientist wasn't he? Should
have known better than that?

GILES : Well, his folks claimed the Gas Board
sent someone round to check the place out but
of course the buggers claimed they knew nothing
about it - bloody computers.

(PAUSE)

MARTIN : Been back to the school recently?

GILES : Yes, all changed - bloody namby-pamby
mob in charge - too damn pink by half. All
the old traditions are going - no more fagging -
no more beatings - they don't even 'Welcome'
the new 'uns anymore - hey, didn't I 'Welcome'
you?

MARTIN : You and a few others.

GILES : Yes I remember, old Dog's Breath and
I pulled you out of bed.

MARTIN : Ashley pulled off my pyjamas and
then Homewood, er Large Arse, branded me with
a cigarette lighter.

GILES : God, yes, and you bit my finger, you
little bugger, so we held you under a bath
for a few minutes.

MARTIN : I nearly drowned. (POURS SOME MORE
DRINK)

GILES : No, really mustn't have any more. Those were the days, eh? Didn't do you any harm did it? You've grown into a really decent chap.

MARTIN : If you say so.

GILES : I know so, old boy, I know so - still must be off, the mem'sahib will be wondering where I've got to - must meet again soon.

MARTIN : Yes, sure. (GILES GETS UP AND MAKES FOR THE DOOR) Go carefully with those brakes!

7 `NEW MANAGEMENT`

by

Jim Tysoe

(NORMAN CUTTING IS DEPUTY ASSISTANT TO THE ASSISTANT HEAD OF EXTERNAL COMMUNICATIONS. HE IS A FADED MAN IN A FADED SUIT. ON A DAY LATE IN HIS UNDISTINGUISHED CAREER, HE IS CHECKING THROUGH A TECHNICAL AREA. HE HAS A CLIPBOARD AND AN INVENTORY. HE IS CONTENT THAT EVERYTHING IS IN ITS PLACE. THERE IS A CRASH [OFF-SCREEN]

JOE (V/O): Oh, damn!

(NORMAN RUSHES ROUND THE CORNER TO SEE JOE, A YOUNG MAN IN T-SHIRT AND JEANS, RUTHLESSLY LOADING ENGINEERING JUNK INTO A TEA CHEST. JOE HAS A CROWBAR AND OTHER WEAPONS OF DESTRUCTION. NORMAN RUNS INTO VIEW)

NORMAN: Just what the devil do you think you're doing? Put that down! (HE LOOKS AROUND) My God, you've wrecked the place!

JOE: Oh yeah, I do a good job.

NORMAN: Just you wait, just you wait right here. (HE MOVES OFF)

JOE: (CALLING AFTER HIM) O.K. guv - but don't be long, I've got the conference rooms to rip out before knocking-off time!

NORMAN: I said stay right there. If you touch anything, anything at all, it'll be the worse for you. I'm going for Security.

(NORMAN WALKS OFF, TURNS A CORNER AND COLLIDES WITH JOE WHO APPEARS AS IF BY MAGIC FROM THE OPPOSITE DIRECTION)

JOE: You rang, Sir?

NORMAN: Get out of my way.

JOE: You wanted the security person. Well, here I am. How's that for service?

NORMAN: I warn you, I'm in no mood for jokes.

JOE: I'm not joking, honest. (HE FLASHES A SECURITY CARD/BADGE)

NORMAN: The world's gone mad. I... I... I think I'm going to need one of my pills. (HE FUMBLES IN HIS POCKET FOR A BOTTLE)

JOE: Executive stress, we were taught the symptom on our first-aid course. You are a classic case. You should sit down.

NORMAN: I have no intention of sitting down. I will not be diverted from my purpose.

JOE: You'd feel better.

NORMAN: I'm alright.

JOE: You don't look it. You look stressed.

NORMAN: I don't.

JOE: Do.

NORMAN: Don't.

JOE: Do.

NORMAN: Listen you bloody vandal, (SHOUTING) I am not stressed!!! (HE HAS A NEAR-BLACKOUT) Oh my God, I'm going to have to sit down.

(JOE GOES TO HELP HIM)

NORMAN: Stay away from me!

JOE: If you don't behave yourself I shall have to use restraint.

NORMAN: Now look!

JOE: (VERY COMMANDING) Shut up! (NORMAN OBEYS) That's better. 'Cannot accept change' - I'm afraid I'll have to file a report. I'll advise a sympathetic response of course.

NORMAN: Now just you listen to me. I'm not sure exactly what is happening. I'm probably about to wake up and find **Hermionie** snoring in my ear, but if this is the real world then this is the engineering nerve centre. I am the Deputy Assistant to the Assistant Head and you are a hooligan who I caught red-handed rendering the disused plant useless!

JOE: There is of course a simple explanation.

NORMAN: I'm all ears.

JOE: Private tender, functions have been combined. Now I work for 'Firm Hands Ltd' and we are pleased to provide minimal security at a very considerable cost.

NORMAN: Then what possible advantage can there be?

JOE: By combining the role of vandal and security person we minimise loss. The management can accurately predict its replacement requirements. I expect I could help your department no end. I bet there's a lot of equipment you'd like to replace.

NORMAN: Well, of course there is, but...

JOE: Just say the word and I'll smash it up - tactfully of course, in the small hours, like.

NORMAN: If you expect me to believe this you must...

JOE: How do you think catering got their new kitchen? Remember that outbreak of salmonella? Very economic!

NORMAN: Economic! Those new kitchens cost a fortune, and three people died

JOE: Exactly, the expense was justified. That's all that matters you see.

NORMAN: The management knew? You're telling me they knew?

JOE: They were reticent at first, but then 'Firm Hands' came with such impressive references. British Rail was our first big client. **Then** Yugo Tours. A final solution to their over-booking problems but I think it was our combined contract with the Department of the Environment and British Nuclear Fuels that clinched the deal here.

(NORMAN MAKES A DASH TO A DISTANT PHONE. JOE OBSERVES HIM CYNICALLY)

NORMAN: Hello, Mr Pearson, it's Cutting here. Norman Cutting. Yes, your assistant. Alright, your deputy assistant. Look, I'm in the main store and there's this vandal who... No, no, I... yes, but...but you don't... (NORMAN PUTS THE PHONE DOWN AND LOOKS SHATTERED)

NORMAN: He said, he said that I should assist you. That I should assist you!

(NORMAN RIPS THE   PHONE OFF THE WALL AND SMASHES IT)

JOE: You shouldn't have done that. (NORMAN GRUNTS) The phones aren't due for replacement until the autumn. I'm afraid you'll have to come along with me.

8 `THE PROCESS`

by

Mike Crisp

(RON, A MAN IN HIS LATE FORTIES/LATE FIFTIES
WAKES UP IN A RATHER TATTY BED - HE IS WEARING
OLD-**FASHIONED PYJAMAS**. THE ROOM IS A VOID,IT
HAS NO REAL FEATURES (BLACKS?). FRED LOOKS
PUZZLED. HE FEELS HE SHOULD BE IN PAIN BUT
DECIDES THAT HE ISN'T - THIS COMES AS ALMOST A
SUPRISE.
A BRIGHT LIGHT HITS HIM AS THE DOOR OPENS AND
A YOUNG MAN ENTERS. HE IS SCRUFFILY DRESSED
BUT NOT TOO PUNK. AGED ABOUT 24. HE DOESN'T
LOOK VERY WELL. HIS NAME IS PETER)

PETE: You still here then, Ron?

RON: Who are you? How do you know my name?
Where is this?

PETE: My name's Pete. You're Ron Simpson,
you told me that when you arrived, don't you
remember?

RON: I don't remember anything - I don't
remember them bringing me here that's for
sure.

PETE: You came here by yourself.

RON: Don't be daft. I only had the operation yesterday - where's Mary?

PETE: She your wife?

RON: Yes.

PETE: I expect she's sitting by the bed holding your hand.

RON: You are daft. (A STRONG LIGHT HITS RON AND HE SCREWS UP HIS EYES - **QUICK CUT** - A JACKET BEING HUNG ON A RAIL AND A PRICE TAG PINNED ON THE SLEEVE - **CUT BACK TO RON**) Oh bugger, I thought I was getting better.

PETE: What's up?

RON: I've started to imagine things - stupid things.

PETE: Like what?

RON: My best jacket in a second-hand shop - and yesterday I saw our Darren driving my car - I imagined it like, I mean I never let the little sod near my car.

PETE: But now he's driving it - that's really funny. (HE CHUCKLES)

RON: No, it isn't, it's a pain in the arse - I felt better this morning but now I've got hallucinations.

PETE: They're not hallucinations.

RON: What?   What do you know about it anyway?   Look, who the hell are you?

PETE: I told you I'm Pete - and you're Ron - you came here last night but you've not been processed yet, that's why you're seeing things.
(THE BRIGHT LIGHT AGAIN - SHOTS OF 'CAR FOR SALE', 'HOUSE FOR SALE' (STILLS?), RON'S PHOTO IN A SILVER FRAME BEING DUSTED (OR IMAGES TO BE DECIDED))

RON: Oh My God! - I <u>am</u>, I'm going barmy. (HE IS VERY UPSET)

PETE: (SYMPATHETIC)   It'll   be   alright, really.   I get them as well, honest - Someone else sleeping in my room - My brother buggering up my hi-fi.   Mum finding my porn collection - some are really funny - I love the look on that policeman's face when the Inspector told him he'd hit me too hard - I see that one often.

RON: So, you're in trouble, I knew it. I'm not sharing with a bloody hooligan - it's not right.

PETE: I'm not in trouble,   not any more, not here.

RON: I'm going to complain. It's a bloody disgrace.
(RON GOES TO THE DOOR AND AS HE OPENS IT HE IS BLINDED BY THE LIGHT - THERE IS ANOTHER MONTAGE OF THE IMAGES AS SEEN BEFORE - THE COAT, THE HOUSE FOR SALE, THE CAR, ETC. AND THIS TIME A DISTANT VOICE-OVER)

V/O: We're doing all we can Mrs Simpson. But you must be prepared. He is very weak.
CUT BACK TO 'NORMAL'

PETE: I told you it's no good. We can't go anywhere till we're processed - can't go back, can't go on...

RON: Mary! Mary!

PETE: Does she love you?

RON: Yes, and she's my wife and I love her.

PETE: You'll probably go back then - have a few more good years, eh? IF I go back it'll just be shit like it always was - I'm better off here. (HE GOES TOWARDS THE DOOR)

RON: Don't leave me alone, Pete.

PETE: You'll be alright - you go back to Mary - you'll see me again - there'll be another jacket in the Oxfam shop, a smaller house for sale - you'll see me again - when you understand.

(HE GOES THROUGH THE DOOR TO A BLINDING LIGHT)

V/O(1): Good news, Mrs Simpson, There's a slight improvement in your husband's condition...

V/O(2): Blimey, Sarg, I think you've killed the little sod.

9 'THE APPRENTICE'

by

Mike Crisp

EXT. A SCHOOL YARD (GRANGE HILL SET
                      ELSTREE)

            (MRS WHITE, AN ESTABLISHED
            TEACHER, CROSSES THE YARD ON
            HER WAY TO THE BIKE STALLS,
            SHE HAS A NUMBER OF MATHS
            EXERCISE BOOKS FOR MARKING
            UNDER HER ARM.

            AS SHE PASSES THE FIRE ESCAPE
            SHE IS AWARE OF A YOUNG MAN
            AT THE TOP. SHE TURNS
            SUDDENLY AND HE IS JUST TOO
            SLOW DUCKING BACK TO ESCAPE
            HER NOTICE.)

MRS WHITE: Come down here - come down

this minute.

            (NICK,A YOUNG MAN ABOUT 22,
              COMES DOWN THE FIRE ESCAPE)

MRS WHITE: What are you doing up the

fire escape? Don't you know it's out

of bounds?

NICK: I'm not a pupil, I've left.

MRS WHITE: That makes no difference
   (LOOKS AT HIM MORE CLOSELY)
I used to teach you, didn't I?
You're Roger Hawkins.

NICK: Yes and no.

MRS WHITE: What?

NICK: Yes you used to teach me and
no, I'm not Roger Hawkins. I'm
Nick Turner.

MRS WHITE: Still as cheeky as ever, I
see.

NICK: That's typical. That's a really
typical teacher's remark. One minute
you don't even know who I bleedin' well
am and the next you're patronising me
with some worn-out old cliché.

MRS WHITE: Patronising - that's a big
word for you.

NICK: For who? Roger or Nick?
Any rate I know a lot of big words now -
like huge.

(MRS WHITE STARTS OFF AGAIN TOWARDS
THE BIKE STALLS - NICK FOLLOWS)

MRS WHITE: What are you doing here
anyway?

NICK: I came to see the ice cream man.

MRS WHITE: I presume you mean Mr Walls?

NICK: You know I mean Mr Walls.

MRS WHITE: You still haven't explained
what you were doing up the fire escape.

NICK: I went to see the Headmaster and
took the well-known short cut from his
study down to the school yard. OK?

(THEY HAVE REACHED THE BIKES)
MRS WHITE: Here, make yourself useful.

(SHE HANDS NICK THE EXERCISE BOOKS
AND LOOKS IN HER HANDBAG)
Oh, don't say I've lost it again.

(CONTINUING - ALMOST TO HERSELF)

I've got a piece of paper in here with
the number written on.

NICK: The number?

MRS WHITE: The combination lock for
my bike.

NICK: You should remember it.

MRS WHITE: It doesn't seem to sink in -
I'm hopeless with names and numbers.
  (SHE STARTS TO FIDDLE WITH THE
   COMBINATION LOCK)

 (NICK LOOKS DOWN AND NOTICES THAT THE
  BOOKS HE IS HOLDING ARE MATHS BOOKS.
  MRS WHITE STRUGGLES ON)

NICK: Do you want me to have a go?

MRS WHITE: There's no point without
the number.

NICK: (BRUSHING HER ASIDE) Come on,
I'll do it.   (HE GIVES HER THE BOOKS
AND THEN STARTS TO WORK ON FINDING THE
COMBINATION - HE CONCENTRATES)

NICK: That's one of 'em,it's a 7. Does
that ring a bell?

MRS WHITE: I think so,7,yes - oh I
don't know.

NICK: A 5?

MRS WHITE: Yes, yes I think so.
Why did you want to see Mr Walls?

NICK: I wanted a headmaster's reference.

MRS WHITE: Did he remember you?

NICK: Yes.

MRS WHITE: Oh good.

NICK: No,it wasn't. He didn't give me
the reference - because he remembered
me.

NICK: (HE SUCCEEDS IN OPENING THE LOCK
There you are 57683. (OR WHATEVER)
Now write it down!

MRS WHITE: Thanks.
(SHE STARTS TO WHEEL HER BIKE AWAY
AND NICK WALKS WITH HER)

MRS WHITE: What job were you after?

NICK: You know Bensons the locksmith
in the High Street? They want an
apprentice. I was hoping to become a
Youth Apprentice Person.'Y.A.P.' is,
I believe, the favoured mnemonic - but
no reference,no job.

MRS WHITE: You're obviously good with
locks.

NICK: A vocation,you could say.

MRS WHITE: I'll give you a reference
if you like.

NICK: Would you?

MRS WHITE: One good turn,etc. etc.

NICK: And you'll get the name right -
send it to the right firm, all these
little details correct**?**

MRS WHITE: Yes.

NICK: Mrs White, I love you.
  (HE KISSES HER AND RUNS BACK TOWARDS
   THE FIRE ESCAPE)

MRS WHITE: Where are you going?

NICK: If you're going to give me a
reference I can release Mr Walls.

MRS WHITE: What!

NICK: I locked him in the stationery
cupboard to help him think it over.
  (PRODUCES A SKELETON KEY)

10 '<u>MOMENTS TO GO</u>'

by

Michael Norman

(THERE IS A SOUND OF RIOT, POLICE SIRENS PERHAPS SPORADIC GUN-FIRE. LUKE, A YOUNG BOY, DASHES UP THE STEPS OF AN OFFICE BLOCK, SEVERAL PEOPLE RUSH PAST HIM IN THE OPPOSITE DIRECTION. AT THE TOP OF THE STAIRS HE BLUNDERS INTO A SMART WAITING AREA WHICH HAS AN AIR OF BEING HURRIEDLY VACATED. HANDBAGS, BRIEFCASES, ETC. LEFT LYING ABOUT. LUKE IS SCRUFFY, IT LOOKS AS THOUGH HE'S BEEN IN A FIGHT. HE CARRIES THE HARVEST OF SOME MINOR LOOTING - A BOTTLE OF SPIRITS, SOME TINS OF FOOD, ETC. HE NOTICES IRIS, AN UPPER MIDDLE-CLASS WOMAN IN HER THIRTIES. SHE IS SITTING UPRIGHT AND MOTIONLESS AT THE END OF THE ROOM. THERE IS A MOMENT AS LUKE OBSERVES HER)

<u>IRIS</u>: It won't be safe here.

<u>LUKE</u>: I don't care.

<u>IRIS</u>: I don't want you here, get out. (HER TEMPER RISES) Go on, get out!

<u>LUKE</u>: This your office then?

IRIS: It's Dr Mackenzie's waiting room, he's a psychiatrist, he's my psychiatrist.

LUKE: Is he still here then?

IRIS: I've got an appointment. I've got every right to be here.

(LUKE TAKES A SWIG FROM HIS BOTTLE OF LOOTED SCOTCH)

LUKE: Are you off your trolley then?

IRIS: Dr Mackenzie says I was suffering from stress.   But I'm better now, much better than I was. (SOME HEAVY GUN-FIRE   ON   THE   SOUND TRACK) Oh my God, it's getting worse!

LUKE: Here, have some of this.(HE GETS CLOSE TO IRIS FOR THE FIRST TIME AND OFFERS HER HIS BOTTLE OF SCOTCH)

IRIS: You looted that, didn't you?

LUKE: Yes.

IRIS: Then I'd rather not, thank you.

LUKE: Please yourself. It'll make it easier, though.

IRIS: Some people still have standards. If more people had standards we wouldn't have got into this shambles.

LUKE: I got this off a policeman. He was carrying so much he tripped over.

IRIS: Who's doing the shooting?

LUKE: Everyone. The looters, the police and there's some evil-looking gits I'd never seen before - Emergency Control Squads or something.

IRIS: I think it's disgraceful. A time of national crisis and people behaving like animals. You think it's clever, I suppose?

LUKE: What the fuck do you expect? Did you really think that everyone would go home, take their doors off and build a shelter in the front room - surrounding themselves with enough plastic bags to wrap the corpses in? You know what I hope? I hope the fucking bomb lands right on the top of this building, that's what I hope.

IRIS: So do I. Oh, so do I.(SHE STARTS TO CRY).

LUKE: Here have some, go on you'll feel better. (HE OFFERS HER THE BOTTLE AGAIN - IRIS TAKES A GOOD SWIG)

IRIS: Not used to alcohol.

LUKE: I'm getting you into bad habits. Funny, if I got caught stealing again they'd put me away from a long time. (TO IMPRESS HER) I've got a suspended sentence, you know.

IRIS: If you were looting you could've been shot.

LUKE: Wouldn't make much difference now would it?

IRIS: No - I was getting better you know, Dr Mackenzie said I was getting better. Mother died, you see, and I didn't seem to be able to cope. We'd been very close, Mummy and I.

LUKE: I never knew my Mum, she buggered off when I was two.

(PAUSE)

IRIS: What's your name?

LUKE: Luke.

IRIS: I'm Iris.

LUKE: (RATHER FORMALLY) Pleased to meet you. (THEY SHAKE HANDS AND REMAIN HOLDING HANDS FOR A MOMENT, THEN LUKE BREAKS AWAY TOWARDS THE WINDOW)

LUKE: It's gone quiet outside - do you think that means-? Oh God, I'm scared. (HE TAKES A BIG SWIG FROM THE BOTTLE)

IRIS: You shouldn't drink like that, it's not good for you. (SHE REALISES WHAT SHE'S SAID AND THEY BOTH LAUGH)

LUKE: What's the time?

IRIS: Five to three.

LUKE: Any minute now, then.

(PAUSE)

IRIS: I never did see 'Swan Lake'.

LUKE: What?

IRIS: 'Swan Lake', it's a ballet - we were going to see it one Christmas when I was about twelve. Mummy and Daddy and I. Daddy was still alive then, you see. Any rate, I got mumps so that spoilt it for everyone. Dad said he'd get some more tickets but he never did - he became ill, you see, very ill, so we never went.

LUKE: I never had me own bike - I pinched a few of course, but it ain't the same is it?

IRIS: What's that?

(THERE IS AN INCREASINGLY THREATENING DRONE ON THE SOUND TRACK)

LUKE: I dunno. Must be the bomber or the missile or whatever the bloody thing is.

IRIS: Hold on to me, Luke. Please! (LUKE HOLDS HER AND THEN KISSES HER)

LUKE: It's quiet in here - we're safe in here.

2 Glossary

The film and television industry has its own vocabulary which itself is littered with abbreviations and slang. The following list is by no means comprehensive but it does contain some useful more commonly heard words and phrases.

Action	The universal cue command to actors. It is what they want to hear, don't be afraid to use it.
AD	Assistant Director, 1st, 2nd and 3rd. Spanning a range of great responsibility from second in command to dog's body.
Anti-flare	Aerosol spray used to dull reflective surfaces.
Aperture	The iris which controls the amount of light that strikes the film or electronic chip.
Aspheron	Supplementary lens providing relatively undistorted extreme wide angle (as long as you don't pan).
Autocue	Trade name for a device which reflects the words to be spoken by a presenter into a half-silvered mirror mounted in front of the lens. The result is that the presenter can clearly see to read words which are invisible to the camera.
AVID	An American non-linear video editing system used for video or film editing (after transfer from the negative).
Baby legs	Small tripod for low angles.
Back projection	System to provide moving background by projecting a film on a giant screen behind the subject. Much used in black and white films, is less convincing in colour.
Backstory (US)	The character's biography prior to start of the script.
Barn door	Hinged black metal masking on the front of a light.
'Bathroom'	Old term for the addition of echo.

Bazooka	Camera pedestal mount useful in confined spaces. Also strong enough to support a jib.
BCU	Big close-up.
Best boy	Second in command of electricians (sometimes 'grips' (US)).
Betacam	Popular professional video format.
Blimp	Soundproofing for the film camera. Usually a specially made case.
Block	(*Verb*) Setting the actors' moves within a scene. (*Noun*) A piece of wood used to add extra height to a piece of furniture.
Blond	2-kilowatt (kW) general-purpose lamp.
Board	Abbreviation for clapper board.
Boom	Mechanical extending arm on which a microphone is mounted.
Brute	Huge arc lamps requiring direct current and a lot of attention. Now largely defunct but still loved by some senior lighting directors.
Bubble	Slang term for the bulb inside any type of film lamp.
Buzz track	Wild track of the atmosphere at any particular location.
Charlie bar	Long, thin 'flags' (see *flag*).
Clapperboard	Small black board with top-hinged bar which claps shut to provide a synch reference. The clapperboard thus provides aural and visual identification for each shot.
Colour temp.	The colour bias of any light source (i.e. daylight is blue or cold – tungsten is reddish or warm).
CU	Close-up.
DAT	Digital audio tape which has now almost entirely re-placed quarter-inch tape for location sound recording.
Day for night	Technique for filming in sunlight and making it look like moonlight, only really successful in black and white where the sky can be blackened by use of a red filter.
Depth of field	The distance before and behind the subject that remains in focus. It varies depending on the lens in use and the aperture.
DFI	Different F … idea – often heard muttered when the director changes his mind after a long time has been expended on his first intention.
Diffusion filter	Various grades of glass 'misting' to soften the image. Strong grades sometimes called fog filters
DIN	German standard for measuring the sensitivity of film to light.

Dioptre	A supplementary lens which allows the lens to which it is fitted to focus on very small, near objects.
Distagon	Range of exceptional quality prime lenses all of which can open to unusually wide apertures and are thus often used in low-light conditions.
Dissolve	Old term for a picture mix.
Dolly	General term for any camera-tracking device. Also verb 'dolly left', etc.
Dougal	A fleecy wind gag for a microphone (which makes it look like Dougal the dog from 'The Magic Roundabout').
Dub	The final sound mix – not merely the approximate revoicing of dialogue into another language.
Dutch take	A 'pretend' take. The person in front of the camera believes it to be real but the camera is not running. Also 'strawberry filter'.
DVE	Digital video effect. There is a host of miraculous computer-driven devices now available to create visual effects. Each has its own acronym, e.g. 'harry', 'charisma', etc. and each is capable of making the image vanish up its own trouser leg.
Eastmancolor	The negative film stock available in various speeds for professional use.
Elbow	To cancel or leave out.
Elephant's foot	A block approx. 1 ft tall constructed like a large hoof. Used to support tracks on very uneven ground, sometimes stood on by cameramen in need of extra height.
Elemac	Second-league tracking device with electrically operated jib.
End board	The use of the clapperboard at the end of the shot for which it is held upside down. Used often in documentaries or when a front board would be unwise (e.g. would 'spook' the horse).
Filter	Any additional piece of glass attached in front of the lens. They can alter the colour, exposure and texture of the image – many and various.
Fish eye	Extreme wide-angle lens.
Fish pole	A long rod to which the microphone is attached for drama sound recording. Operated by the assistant sound recordist and turning him into a 'human boom'.
Flag	A piece of black board placed in front of a light to shadow off some of its beam.
Flood	(*Verb*) To widen the spread of a light.
Focus pulling	Changing the focus setting during filming to keep

the subject sharp as it moves – or sometimes dramatically altering the centre of attention within a shot.

Follow focus
A gear system linked to a large knob which connects with the lens and simplifies the process of focus pulling.

FPS
Frames per second.

French flag
A small flag attached by a flexible bar to the camera and used to shield the lens from unwanted reflections, sun, etc.

Fresnel lens
A piece of glass fitted to certain lights to provide a focused beam, i.e. one that will give distinct shadows.

Front projection
Convincing method of combining studio foreground with prefilmed background. A glass-beaded screen reflects the image from the projector straight into the camera lens but deflects any other light that strikes it. Therefore the lighting of the studio subject does not spoil the image in the same way as it does with back projection. Front projection works well with colour and was used with spectacular success in Stanley Kubrick's '2001'.

FX
Slang for 'effects'.

Gaffer
Chief electrician.

Genny
Generator to supply location power.

Glass shot
Old film method of supplying false scenery by painting details (the castle on the hill) on a large piece of glass in front of the camera.

Gobo
A cut-out mask placed in front of a light to provide a specific shadow effect – prison bars, venetian blind, etc.

Grips
The technician responsible for tracking, tracking equipment and special mounts.

Guide track
Synchronous sound recorded to aid post-synchronization.

Gun mic
Highly directional microphone.

HMI
Family of lights ranging from 2 kW to 16 kW which run on 110 volts AC. They have a colour temperature very close to daylight and all have fresnel lenses to provide a focused beam.

ISO
International Standards Organization. The most common scale against which film's sensitivity to light is measured (125 ISO, 400 ISO, etc.).

Jensen interlock
Device to synchronize a film camera with a TV screen (and thus avoid black bars across the television picture).

Jib	A counter-balanced swivel arm camera mount enabling elegant camera moves.
Kitten	1-kW lamp with fresnel lens.
Kodachrome	A reversal colour film which provides beautiful results. The difficulty in copying from it has largely restricted its use to the amateur world.
Kodak	The invented brand name of the Eastman Film Company.
Latitude	The capacity of a film stock to be wrongly exposed yet still print OK.
Light beam	A sectional beam that can be fitted across the top of a room and support a considerable number of lights.
Light works	A British non-linear video editing system now used for off-line editing of video or (after transfer) film.
Lightning strike	Modern device to provide realistic lightning from a 110 volts AC source.
Long-focus lens	A lens which magnifies the image.
M&E	Music and effects track.
Matt box	A bellows-like casing which fits on to the front of the camera and shields the lens from lighting 'flares'. It also may hold filters and masks (such as telescope or keyhole) that may be required.
Matt shot	A process to combine two separately exposed images (actors in car and moving background).
MCU	Medium close-up.
Mizar	The smallest focusing lamp (350 watts).
'Mole'	Short for Mole Richardson, trade name of large crane.
Monochrome	One colour or, more simply, black and white. Old B/W film was more sensitive to blue than other colours. Later panchromatic stocks became available which rendered the different colours as varying degrees of grey. True black and white is now difficult to get processed in the UK.
Moonbeam	An all-in-one generator and hoist which allows a powerful lamp (12 kW) to be skied to provide the effect of moonlight.
Moviola	Another US trade name. The company is best known for film-editing machines and also dollies, both of which are known as 'Moviolas'.
Moy head	A geared camera mount which pans and tilts the camera by the winding of two separate handles. It takes time to acquire the skill to operate it but provides exceptionally smooth camera moves and is essential for the larger feature cameras.

MS	Mid-shot.
Mute shot	To film a shot with no sound.
Nagra	Very high quality battery-driven reel-to-reel tape recorder still preferred by recordists working in remote regions – as they are easier to repair than DAT recorders.
ND	A filter which reduces the amount of light passing through the lens without affecting the colour.
Neon light	Neon lights as used in offices, etc. provide a very unpleasant greeny blue image on film and video. Some film stocks are available which cope better than the standard ones. Also replacement tubes which are more akin to daylight can be used.
Off-line	Any video editing system which provides a work copy which will subsequently need to be remade to broadcast standard.
On-line	Video editing to broadcast standard.
Operator	On a film the person who actually operates the camera. Seldom the director of photography (who decides on the lighting, lenses and composition of the shot in advance).
Overcrank	To film at more than 24/25 frames per second and thus slow the action down.
Pan	A shot during which the camera rotates on its axis left or right. Up-and-down movement is more properly described as a tilt.
Pan glass	A viewing filter which provides some idea of how the contrast of a scene will appear on film.
Panther	Sophisticated German dolly with electronic jib built in.
Peewee	American dolly, very versatile.
Playback	System to play back music in synchronization with the film or video camera. Much simplified by the arrival of DAT.
Pole cat	Spring-loaded pole which can support a few lights across the tops of passages, etc.
Poly	Sheets of white polystyrene used to reflect light and thus provide a soft overall luminance.
POV	Point of view.
Pre-mix	A combination of some of the tracks that require to be combined in a final sound mix. The purpose is to make the final mixing process more simple by first reducing three or four tracks to one pre-mix.
Prime lens	A lens of fixed focal length. To change the image size you either have to change the position of the camera or change the lens to one of a different

	focal length. Prime lenses provide the best-quality images.
'Pup'	A 2-kW lamp with fresnel lens.
'Rehearse on film'	Sometimes when a shot is very simple for actor and crew it is attempted without rehearsal or 'rehearsal on film'.
Reversal film	Film which, once run through the camera, is developed straight away to a positive image. It has no negative and once damaged there is nothing that can be done. Now very much the province of amateur film makers it was once used by news cameramen. It requires more careful exposure than negative/positive film. All reversal films end in *chrome* (e.g. Kodachrome, Fujichrome). All negative/positive films end in *colour* (e.g. Eastmancolor, Agfacolour).
Reverse action	Staging action backwards which would be dangerous or impossible to perform forwards, i.e. the arrow is pulled *out* of the cowboy's shoulder and the shot is printed backwards to look as though it was shot into him.
Scrim	Spun fibreglass used to diffuse light.
Slate	The board held in front of the camera (clapperboard) at the start of every shot. Each shot has a shot number which refers to its chronological appearance in the script and a slate number which ascends in the order in which the shots are actually taken.
'Soft'	Slightly out of focus.
Speed	The sensitivity of film to light ('fast' film is more sensitive than 'slow').
Spot	(*Verb*) To reduce the spread and thus intensify the beam from a lamp.
Spot effect	Sound effect recorded separately from the picture but whose use requires exact synchronization with the film (gunshots, door slams, etc.).
Stagger	Low-key run-through of a scene for the benefit of camera and sound.
Standard lens	On a still camera of any given format, is the one that takes in more or less the stereoscopic view seen by our two eyes as they work together. The standard lens reproduces the size relationships in depth as seen in that area of stereoscopic vision. Movie cameras have traditionally been fitted with lenses of slightly narrower angle of view than still cameras mainly because the viewer of the fleeting

images of the cinema needs more close-ups and details than the viewer of a fixed, still image. The 'understated' view of the standard lens still remains important in the age of the zoom.

Steadicam	A camera mount which is worn by the operator. It is gyroscopically damped to smooth out bumps and allow for complicated tracking movement.
Strike	To remove a piece of furniture (also to light up an arc lamp).
Super 16 mm	A wide-screen (16 × 9) format achieved by allowing the picture area to spread into that part of the standard 16 mm frame previously reserved for the optical or magnetic sound track. Now in common use for TV film drama.
Supplementary lens	A lens which fits in front of an existing lens and alters its focal length or minimum focus (such as a dioptre).
Take	An attempt to film a shot. The successful attempt is a good take.
Telecine	Device for transferring film to videotape.
Telephoto	An extreme long-focus lens.
Top hat	Lowest camera mount that can still take a pan/tilt head.
Track	A move made by a camera. Towards or away from the subject is to track in and track out, respectively. Also the rails on which the dolly travels.
Tripod	Three-legged universal static camera mount.
Tromboning	Countertracking or zooming in and out too fast.
Tungsten light	Any lamp with a tungsten filament produces a very orange light. Film for use under tungsten light (most professional film) therefore is especially blue-sensitive. Such film, when used in daylight, requires an orange filter to correct this oversensitivity to blue – and as the filter itself absorbs some light, tungsten film is less sensitive to daylight than to artificial light (see colour temp. and Wratten).
.Ulcer	Unpleasantly graphic description of a large fretwork gobo used to create shadows from the most powerful lamps, 12 kWs, brutes, etc. Often used on night shoots.
Ulti matt	Video computer device for combining images, changing backgrounds, etc.
Undercrank	To film at fewer than 24/25 frames per second and thus speed the action up.
UV filter	Filter used at high altitudes to filter out ultraviolet light which would otherwise cause a 'blue cast' on the film.

Wide-screen	There have been many systems in the history of the cinema of which Cinemascope is the most famous. Wide-screen video is now available in Beta format and wide-screen television has arrived and is more common in Europe than the UK. Wide-screen video can only be transmitted 16 × 9. Wide-screen film can be transmitted in aspect ratios other than the one in which it was originally produced.
Wide-angle	A lens which provides a wider view of the scene than the human eye.
White balance	The circuitry in a video camera which colour corrects the image for the prevailing light source. By showing the camera something white the camera decides if the light is tungsten or daylight.
Wild track	Sound taken independently of the picture for inclusion at the final mix.
Wipe	One picture replaces another by pushing it across the frame.
Wrap	'Wind, roll and print' used to be said at the end of a day's filming. Now this is reduced to 'wrap'.
Wratten	Filter manufacturing company; but the term is generally used to describe the filter No. 85 which is required when film colour balanced for tungsten light is exposed in daylight.
Xenon arc	Lamps now commonly used in projectors. Extremely expensive but excellent in operation.
Zoom lens	A lens of variable focal length.
Zoom ratio	The ratio between the shortest and longest focal length of a given zoom lens. For example, a lens which can zoom from 10 mm:100 mm has a ratio of 10 to 1.

Index